THE CHAMPIONSHIPS WIMBLEDON

Official Annual 1991

JOHN PARSONS

Photographs by
BOB MARTIN, SIMON BRUTY and RUSSELL CHEYNE

CHAPMANS

First published 1991 by Chapmans Publishers,
141–143 Drury Lane, Covent Garden, London WC2B 5TB

A catalogue record for this book is available from the British
Library.

ISBN 1 85592 532 X

Designed by Philip Mann/Ace Ltd
Produced by Geoff Barlow

Typeset by Dorchester Typesetting Group Ltd, Dorchester
Origination by Studio One Origination Ltd
Printed in Great Britain by Butler & Tanner Ltd, Frome

This book produced with the assistance of Robinsons and Nikon (UK) Limited

FOREWORD

What a Wimbledon we had in 1991 – it could so easily have been one of the less successful. However, with the teamwork of all concerned, those on the courts as well as those working behind the scenes, The Championships became a glorious celebration.

We had a disastrous start, with no play on the Monday, and little play on the Tuesday, Wednesday and Thursday. Only 52 matches were played on the first four days, whereas we normally expect to play over 60 matches on the first day alone. The last match of the first round of the men's singles finished at 7 pm on Saturday. This meant that, without play on the middle Sunday, some players would have to play a singles match every day, and also a doubles match in some cases. Thus, to be fair to the players, we decided to play on the middle Sunday and break with tradition.

This is when everybody turned adversity into triumph. Players, fans, police, security, ball boys and girls, the Club staff, you name it; they did their job and made the day a great carnival occasion. Twenty-five thousand fans came on a first come, first served basis; many queued overnight. What an enthusiastic, well-behaved crowd they were, the tennis *aficionados* of the future, since the average age was a lot younger than usual. For £10 they saw the likes of Gabriela Sabatini, Stefan Edberg, Jimmy Connors and John McEnroe on Centre Court and Court 1, while for £5 they saw Martina Navratilova, Steffi Graf and Ivan Lendl on Court 2 and the other courts. We even had the 'Wimbledon wave' on the Centre Court and Court 1 – and, believe it or not, the Royal Box joined in.

But there were other successes, too. André Agassi won the hearts of the Wimbledon crowd. Jennifer Capriati, at 15, chose the Centre Court at Wimbledon to beat one of the top four players for the first time – Martina Navratilova; what a match that was! Then there was the victory in the semi-final of Michael Stich over Stefan Edberg, who, though not losing his serve once, lost the match 4–6, 7–6, 7–6, 7–6.

It was lovely to see mixed doubles and ladies' doubles won by pairs who had twice previously been runners-up. But I am sure those who were there in glorious sunshine will best remember the two singles finals. Both the play and the weather were a fitting contrast to that first Monday.

Steffi Graf showed some of the brilliance she had consistently maintained in 1988 and 1989 to overcome in three long sets a gritty performance by Gabriela Sabatini. Michael Stich then surprised those who did not know him with his tremendous resilience and character. He defeated Boris Becker on the favourite arena of the latter. It was a day when Michael's serve and backhand return held sway.

I cannot end this preface without thanking everyone for their cheerfulness during the difficult first week. I hope that you will see the happiness and success of the 105th Championships reflected in the prose and pictures that follow.

J.A.H. Curry
Chairman of The All England Club and the Committee of Management of The Lawn Tennis Championships
July 1991

INTRODUCTION

For a time it seemed as if Wimbledon 1991 might become The Championships that would never end. With an average of only 13 matches a day completed over the first four days, and the weather outlook still bleak, tournament Referee, Alan Mills, was calculating that, with a bit of luck, they would be able to play the finals around 12 August, more than a month late.

In the event, the Atlantic jet-stream, which was to blame for keeping the groundstaff and court coverers busier than most of the players during the first week, moved further north, where it should have been. And Wimbledon 1991 was able to end, not only on time, but in marvellous style.

The delays before it was possible for either the men's or ladies' singles events to begin to take shape were all the more frustrating because of the way appetites had been whetted during the build-up to The Championships. In particular one question uppermost in the minds of many was not simply what André Agassi might decide to wear in his first appearance at Wimbledon since 1987 but, far more relevantly, how would he play?

His decision to return to the United States to recover from the bitter blow of losing his third consecutive Grand Slam tournament final at the French Open, just 15 days before the vital transition from clay courts to grass would have to be made, only increased the speculation.

Agassi did not figure highly in the list of favourites at the start of the fortnight. Stefan Edberg, the defending champion, and Boris

Becker, a former champion who had contested the three previous finals, were jointly favoured as the most likely projected winners once again. But there was much sentimental support for Ivan Lendl, making his 12th attempt to achieve what has been termed 'his great obsession'.

Yet there were also others to consider. Pete Sampras, a brilliant serve and volleyer at his best, who had become the youngest winner of the US Open, had been tipped by no less an expert than Fred Perry and Don Budge as having 'the genuine potential of a Wimbledon champion'. Could Goran Ivanisevic, still only 19, recapture the inspiration that made him a thrilling semi-finalist a year earlier, to become more than simply another 'young pretender'? And there was the new German challenger, Michael Stich, eager to maintain his rapid progress to the top during the first half of the year and described by Edberg, prophetically as it transpired, as 'one of the most dangerous men in the draw'.

No one had truly dominated the first six months of the men's tour. Becker had briefly taken the number one ranking from Edberg by winning the Australian Open, but Jim Courier – who did not yet regard himself as a mature Wimbledon challenger – had stolen in on the blind side to win the French Open.

Among the women it was different. Gabriela Sabatini and Monica Seles had surged ahead of Steffi Graf in terms of victories but, four days before Wimbledon was due to begin, Miss Seles, though halfway towards achieving a Grand Slam after her successes at the Australian Open and the French Open, sent word that she would not be playing.

She too had gone home to the United States from Roland Garros but, unlike Agassi, she did not return to Europe. Her sudden and, at the time, not fully explained withdrawal led to a last-minute shuffling of the seeds. Miss Graf, despite the growing anxieties over her form and confidence (after a shattering defeat in Paris), became number one, with a huge burden on her shoulders. Martina Navratilova, the defending champion, whom many felt should have been top seed, seemed to be sitting back quietly confident that she could strike again for a 10th time, after winning again with almost consummate ease at Eastbourne.

The stage was set, therefore, for the 105th occasion of the greatest lawn tennis event in the world. The pages that follow provide the solution to all the many fascinating questions that were waiting to be answered, and illustrate the way some hopes were painfully dashed and others succeeded beyond their wildest dreams.

Yet again Robinsons
lends its services t

Orange Barley Water

o the Centre Court.

Only Nikon.

Number (xxiv)

The player's eye-view of Wimbledon is a familiar sight: cameras as far as the eye can see. And more Nikons than you could shake a racket at.

In fact, 85% of all press photographers choose to shoot on Nikon. Small wonder then, that Nikon was chosen as the official camera at this year's Wimbledon fortnight. And no surprise at all that Nikon is responsible for the world's greatest pictures.

Now you know why we take the world's greatest pictures.

Nikon

THE
CHAMPIONSHIPS
WIMBLEDON

DAYS

1/2

Monday 24 June

Tuesday 25 June

The all-too depressing scene when The Championships were due to begin.

'Cruel' was not a strong enough word to describe the way the weather closed in on Wimbledon on what should have been the opening day of The Championships, to make it black Monday. 'Heartbreaking' would be a more appropriate term, especially for those who had queued overnight, sleeping beneath polythene sheeting, only for the rain to begin just after the gates had opened.

Even so, more than 26,000 spectators, some 2,000 below the crowd limit, thronged the grounds, the stands and the museum, among other places, and many stayed on until early evening, when all hope of play was abandoned. The patience and perseverance of Wimbledon crowds in such circumstances is unrivalled at any other tennis event around the world.

On Court 14, for instance, there was nothing but a brightly coloured sea of umbrellas to be seen for at least two hours, as hundreds sat stoically in the hope, however slim, that somehow the clouds would break and that first Henri Leconte and then John McEnroe, the two players most of them obviously wanted to see, could appear. Sadly, the waiting was all in vain.

For those sheltering in the relative comfort of Centre Court there were a few opportunities to cheer. Jim Courier, the newly crowned champion of the French Open, came out to pose for photographers. Then defending champion, Stefan Edberg, who at least had managed to fit in about 30 minutes' practice before the rain started, sat alongside his coach, Tony Pickard (also Britain's Davis Cup captain), while Britain's director of national training, Richard Lewis, looked towards a more optimistic future for tennis in the country where the game originated, in a public address interview with BBC Radio's Tony Adamson.

On Court 1 one intrepid spectator even persuaded fellow spectators to play charades, while in the various Press rooms another entirely different game was being played, as journalists from all over the world pondered how to fill the acres of space available to record the most important events of the day.

There was some hard news. The Women's Tennis Association, increasingly embarrassed by the lack of clarification from Monica Seles about why she had withdrawn from the tournament, announced that she was being fined 6,000 US dollars; The Lawn Tennis Association revealed that, together with The All England Club and the Sports Council, it would continue to fund the Indoor Tennis Initiative for the building of tennis facilities in inner-city areas for another five years, to the tune of £7.5 million. And one player due to have played that day actually went out of The Championships. Mats Wilander, the former world champion from Sweden, who had been due to play Britain's Danny Sapsford on Court 3, decided there was no chance that the left knee injury he had aggravated at Queen's Club two weeks earlier would improve sufficiently for him to play.

It was 6.45 pm when the 'no play today' announcement finally came, making it the second time in five years that there had been a washout on the first Monday. In fact, detailed records kept by Assistant Referee Tony Gathercole show that in recent years, at least, the first Monday has been the most vulnerable day in terms of weather. Apart from the two completely blank occasions, six other first Mondays have suffered serious disruption of

*Martina Navratilova, the defending champion, went
through the anguish of her toughest first-round
match in 17 years against Elna Reinach.*

Miss Reinach, elegant despite her first-round Centre Court downfall.

play since 1977 (with only one match finished in 1985).

Just to add to the gloom, the weather forecast was that even worse was to come. Record books were quickly consulted and showed that not since 1909, when the first Thursday and Friday of The Championships were lost, had there been two consecutive days without play. One took comfort from the belief that, if nothing else, this would become part of the tournament's history.

The revised Order of Play for Day Two meant that Edberg would no longer open the Centre Court programme, as tradition decrees, but that the privilege would go to Martina Navratilova, the defending ladies' singles champion, as Wimbledon still regards this as Ladies' Day. There was also the added justification that Miss Navratilova, who 12 months earlier had won the singles crown for a record ninth time, was just one victory away from recording her 100th match win at Wimbledon.

Fortunately the weather experts – who had originally predicted that it would be fine until at least late in the afternoon on Monday – were fooled by nature once again, in that on Day Two things were better than expected. It was therefore at 12.46 pm that Halle Cioffi of the United States served the first ball of Wimbledon '91 to the Austrian, Judith Wiesner, on Court 4. Miss Wiesner went on to win, as did all the other women seeds who played that day; but it was only after finding herself six points from defeat that Miss Navratilova weathered her particular first-round storm.

On an occasion when, presumably, both she and most of the crowd expected to celebrate her century of victories – the first in the history of The Championships – in a relaxed, imposing style, she had to survive the toughest first-round fight she had faced in 17 years from the 22-year-old South African, Elna Reinach.

'In the end I just won it on emotion,' said Miss Navratilova, who had often looked frail. Memories of the last time she had been taken to three sets in the first round – by another South African, Tanya Harford, in 1979 – came flooding back, especially at 3–4, 0–30 in the final set, when she was clearly in danger of becoming the first women's singles champion to lose in the first round.

'That wasn't as close as this one,' commented Miss Navratilova. 'I don't think I've ever come back from three breaks in the final set and won. I

Perfect balance and control as Steffi Graf launches her campaign against Sabine Appelmans.

thought I might lose throughout the whole match. That was one of my problems. But I was determined I wasn't going to give up.'

Reinach, a tall, elegant right-hander, who just as often stroked as struck winners to all corners of the court, admitted that she lost 'because, when it came to the crunch, I got scared. Maybe I held back too much.' Indeed, had she more often gone for passing shots, than for lobs which invariably fell short and repeatedly allowed Navratilova to escape further moments of crisis, she probably would have won.

Miss Navratilova, wincing with a mixture of agony and relief as she mentally replayed some of the most crucial moments of a 2 hour 45 minute match, said, 'God, she has the longest arms. I hit the ball past her so many times but all of a sudden it would come back. She has such reach.'

At 3–4, 30–30, Navratilova had the luckiest of escapes. Fending off a second serve into her midriff, she hit an awkward-looking shot, which touched the top of the net and dropped like a stone on Reinach's side. The champion took 12 of the last 13 points, but in 14 of her service games she had either been broken, saved break points or been pressed to deuce. Reinach was not too upset at having let slip her chance. 'It was fun. I'd rather have played Martina on the Centre Court than anyone else on a back court,' she said afterwards.

The promise from Miss Navratilova was 'Believe me, I'm not going to make mistakes like that again', and the person to whom that was immediately of the greatest interest was Britain's Amanda Grunfeld, who, 18 months after a serious back operation, recorded her first win in five attempts at Wimbledon by beating the French player, Alexia Dechaume, 6–4, 6–4.

An even more impressive first-round British victory was recorded on Court 13, where Jo Durie, who has had enough back problems of her own, upset the 22nd-ranked Helen Kelesi from Canada, 6–3, 6–2. But there was domestic disappointment in the crowded narrow corridor alongside Court 4, when Belinda Borneo failed to sustain a 4–0 final-set lead and a point for 5–1, and was beaten 2–6, 6–3, 6–4 by the Bulgarian, Elena Pampoulova.

Steffi Graf, despite six double faults, and Arantxa Sanchez Vicario made almost predictable first-round progress on a day when only 28 matches were completed before the rain returned to London SW19 and it was announced that, for the next few days at least, play would begin on

Marc Rosset was always under pressure in the first round from defending champion, Stefan Edberg.

outside courts at 11 am, and on Centre Court and Court 1 at 1 pm.

Of the men who managed to beat the weather, two were former champions. Pat Cash, the 1987 winner, moved cautiously on Court 1, especially after an hour's disruption, to beat the American left-hander, Jeff Tarango, while John McEnroe looked far more severe as he beat the Brazilian, Jaime Oncins, 6–1, 6–2, 6–4. McEnroe, who had only just made it into the seedings, was helped by 12 double faults from his opponent, including four in one game at 2–2 in the second set. 'I'm assuming he didn't play at his best,' McEnroe observed wryly.

Edberg's opening match, already delayed for more than 24 hours, was first interrupted and then pushed into a third day with him two sets ahead of Marc Rosset, the heavy-serving Swiss player, who held his serve in the opening game of the third. Meanwhile Andrei Cherkasov was within two games of becoming the first seed to be eliminated, by American Richey Reneberg on Court 4, when the court covers had to go back on.

The Championships were under way – but only just.

John McEnroe's early mood tended to match the gloomy weather.

D A Y S
3/4

Wednesday 26 June

Thursday 27 June

Torrential overnight rain, which meant some of the car parking areas were already beginning to resemble sodden, newly ploughed fields, did nothing to dampen the enthusiasm of those who were earliest into The All England Club on Day Three. They were also the lucky ones, for there was just over an hour of play on most outside courts during the long-overdue dry spell – then nothing more until the fine weather being enjoyed all day, barely 25 miles away, spread back to Wimbledon, enabling matches on Centre Court, Court 1 and some of the outside courts to resume after 6.45 pm.

Just five matches were completed in the first period, among them a 6–1, 6–2 victory for Anke Huber, 16, who had left school two weeks earlier and, depending on your point of view, either has to live up to or live down to the tag in her native Germany of being considered 'the next Steffi Graf'. Miss Huber, already among the world's top 20 players, likes Wimbledon but not playing on grass,

Veronika Martinek (inset), pulled out of court and out of the tournament by fellow German, Anke Huber.

24

The Fred Perry statue (top).
Jennifer Capriati (left) made a positive enough start against Shaun Stafford.

Gabriela Sabatini launches into one of her best passing shots, which eventually wore down Britain's Monique Javer.

After a promising first set, Monique Javer was well beaten by Gabriela Sabatini.

Pam Shriver gritted her teeth to beat Andrea Leand.

(Right) The long-awaited, all-white arrival of André Agassi with Grant Connell (top left). Despite an early tumble and loss of the first set, Agassi soon picked himself up to beat the banana-munching Canadian.

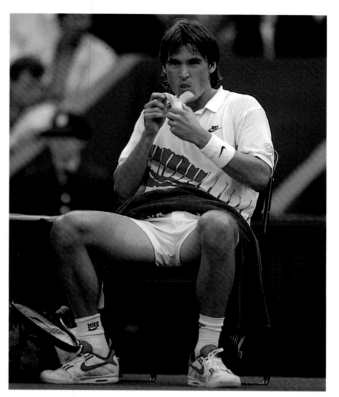

A scoreboard operator makes sure the names are
correctly placed on outside courts.

although her coach, Boris Breskvar, who was also
initially involved in the evolution of the games of
Miss Graf and Boris Becker, believes the latter is
only a temporary phase.

The girl from Karlsburg, which is tucked neatly
between Graf's home town in Bruhl and Becker's
in Leimen, beat fellow German Veronika Martinek
comfortably, but not in the style demanded by
Breskvar. 'If she plays like that again she will not
win the next round,' he said, ordering extra practice for her that afternoon.

Because of the rain, Miss Huber escaped her
punishment. And she was not the only one to find
there was a silver lining to the black clouds. Of the
19 British players originally in the draw (all six of
the men and a majority of the 13 women on wild
cards) several of the 13 still involved in singles at
the end of Day Three had certainly been helped by
the weather to collect their £90 a day expenses
longer than might have been expected.

The most feverish action came towards the end
of yet another mainly damp and frustrating day,
when a further 13 matches were either played or
completed, taking the paltry three-day total to 46
when it should have been around 180. The long-
suffering spectators were rewarded with touches
of colourful brilliance from both Gabriela Sabatini
and Jennifer Capriati.

Miss Sabatini took time to overcome much
dogged and spirited resistance from the British
Californian, Monique Javer, who had a break point
at 2–1, but perhaps the Argentinian's slow start
was not really surprising. She had first appeared
on the Centre Court on schedule for a 1 pm start,
but after only two minutes of the knock-up had to
take refuge in the dressing room. When they tried
again 90 minutes later, the knock-up had lasted
four minutes when the court coverers once more
had to be put through their paces, with the same
efficiency and expertise as the naval gun crews in
competition at the Royal Tournament – and with
the enduring support and admiration of the
crowds.

It was nearly six hours later when Miss
Sabatini made a somewhat gingerly start, but after
an opening set of 43 minutes she produced a

Goran Ivanisevic tried in vain to convince Assistant Referee Tony Gathercole that the court was too slippery.

stunning serve and volley display in the second set for a 6–4, 6–0 victory.

Miss Capriati's method was somewhat different. Playing in what one observer said looked like discarded sailing shorts, but what more fashion-conscious eyes recognized as being culottes, she rampaged through the first set in only 16 minutes against Shaun Stafford, but in the end was more than grateful for her opponent's double fault, which allowed her back into the second set at 2–2 (not to mention another double fault on match point), as she claimed her 6–0, 7–5 win.

Pam Shriver, unseeded for the first time in ten visits, also rattled off her first set in next to no time against another fellow American, Andrea Leand, who, since sensing that her outstanding promise as a junior was not going to be fulfilled, has additionally become a tennis journalist. Shriver won the first set 6–0, but only took the second 7–5 on her fifth match point, after missing the first three at 5–3 and being broken to love at 5–4, thereby at least giving Miss Leand a defiant comeback tale to tell.

Such was the backlog of matches by now, however, that the possibility of having to play on the middle Sunday of The Championships, hitherto regarded as sacrosanct, was being mooted far more seriously than ever before, though two seeds who already knew that it would not concern them, at least not in singles, were Helena Sukova and Andrei Cherkasov.

Cherkasov, who must have been surprised, especially after never having won a match on his three previous Wimbledon visits, to have been seeded 12th – when a genuine, supremely confident serve and volleyer such as David Wheaton, lower-ranked but runner-up at Queen's Club, was not seeded at all – lasted only another eight minutes against Richey Reneberg.

The Russian, who had broken back from 1–4 to 3–4 in the third set before play had been stopped the night before, made it 4–4 but was always struggling. However admirable his attempts to play a serve and volley game were, he lacked both the experience and skill to deal with the power of the American's returns. Reneberg won 6–4, 6–3, 6–4, on a day when the only other man to advance was Derrick Rostagno, who had his own army of admirers as he beat the curly-haired Italian newcomer, Renzo Furlan, 6–0, 6–3, 6–4 in two instalments on Court 10.

Eleven women's matches were decided, and

the last of them brought a 4–6, 6–1, 6–4 defeat for the 10th seed, Helena Sukova (her earliest loss since 1983), by Gigi Fernandez, the United States' Federation Cup player from Puerto Rico who, though only 69th in the world rankings at the time, would be considered one of the top dozen women players on grass. Fernandez, a set down but 3–0 up in the second when play had stopped the night before, was firmly in control when they resumed a match that finally finished in the gloom at 8.25 pm.

On Day Four only another six matches were completed before what the London Weather Centre had suggested would be 'a short, sharp shower' became another deluge, making it, officially, the wettest Wimbledon in the history of a tournament that started in 1877.

Yet for more than an hour, in one of the unfinished matches, the Centre Court was brilliantly illuminated by the all-white appearance of André Agassi and the captivating impression he immediately created. It had been four years since Wimbledon had last seen Agassi; then his visit had been confined to what was, for him, an embarrassingly short, sharp, grass-court lesson from Henri Leconte, who had allowed him only five games on Court 2.

Now, after an interim period of increasing controversy – caused not only by his apparent love for garish clothing but also by his comments on various issues and personalities within the game, and of course by his failure to win any of the last three Grand Slam tournament finals in which he had played in the previous 13 months – he was in the full Centre Court spotlight of an event he had once called 'just another tournament'.

Everyone, it seemed, including guests in the Royal Box, was eager to see what he would be wearing. The public relations men had clearly done a magnificent job. In true showman style he maintained the suspense. After a deep bow to The Duchess of Kent, which he timed rather better than some of his earliest groundstrokes, he kept his all-white tracksuit on throughout the knock-up before revealing, to another round of applause (which provoked a sheepish grin), all-white kit, except for one or two small logos. There was no sign of the denim shorts, though the built-in cycling-style thigh-warmers, also in all-white, were there.

When the match began, Agassi's sorties to the net were few and far between, especially in the first set. The first point, involving 12 strokes, was something of a surprise on grass but underlined the contrasting styles of Agassi and his Canadian opponent, Grant Connell, who until this moment must have felt like little more than an 'extra' on the scene.

Agassi double-faulted twice in his first service game and saved three break points in his second, so it was hardly unexpected when Connell took the first set 6–4. However, with his groundstrokes then starting to flow more easily, and by regularly taking the ball early with a short backswing, Agassi took the next set 6–1, before the storm cut things short, just when it had become so fascinating, at 1–1 in the third.

Earlier, Stefan Edberg had taken just 26 minutes to complete a 6–4, 6–4, 6–4 defeat of the lofty Marc Rosset, but he called it 'the longest match I've ever played', because it finished 72 hours 44 minutes after it should have started on the opening Monday. Rosset had produced 14 aces, one of them timed by the IBM radar gun at 134 miles per hour, which was to remain the fastest of the fortnight on Centre Court. But there were costly double faults in between, while Edberg, who looked in superb form, never lost more than two points on his own service games and won many of them to love.

After two years in which he had lost in the first round, Pete Sampras, the youngest winner of the US Open title in September 1990, was overjoyed at registering his first Wimbledon win with a 6–1, 6–2, 6–2 defeat of Brazil's Danilo Marcelino, making his first visit. But there were more frowns than smiles on Court 1, where Goran Ivanisevic, the 10th seed, briefly staged a sit-down strike as his much-interrupted match with Andrew Castle reached 7–6, 5–5.

Despite their close encounter at Manchester a week earlier, by which time the Wimbledon draw had already been made, Ivanisevic had said that Castle had 'no chance' of beating him. In fact, the first set went to a tie-break in which Castle led 6–3 after a marvellous backhand volley, but then a netted backhand, the 11th ace from Ivanisevic and a full-blooded forehand pass robbed the Englishman of his chance.

It was during the second game of the second set, after a code violation for ball abuse, that Ivanisevic lost his self-control. And when he fell for a third time moments later, he sat by the umpire's chair, protesting that the court was unsafe, until Assistant Referee Tony Gathercole

The umbrellas tell their own story on Court 1 as Andrew Castle's defiant first-round effort against Goran Ivanisevic is interrupted.

told him firmly, 'The court is quite dry – the court is quite playable.'

Castle, clearly hoping to capitalize on the situation, made a gesture resembling a gorilla towards Ivanisevic, which amused the crowd but which the Yugoslavian presumably did not see, for he had efficiently delivered another flurry of aces before another shower made further play impossible.

For the record, Day Four ended with only 52 matches finished, compared with the previous worst figure in modern times of 107 by that stage, in 1987. Happily, as we were soon to discover, the worst at least was over.

D A Y

Friday 28 June

The Wimbledon shop, one of the most popular attractions when there was no tennis to watch, had already sold out of its initial stock of 500 umbrellas – but no matter. Just before 11 am on Day Five, Christopher Gorringe, the tournament's Chief Executive, was able to make the announcement, 'Welcome to a sunny All England Club. Play will begin on all eighteen courts.'

It was the serious beginning of the arduous catching-up process for all concerned, not least for tournament Referee, Alan Mills, and his staff, who had regularly been forced to revise the listings on the Order of Play boards.

On Centre Court, not used to such activity at 11 am, The All England Club Chairman, John Curry, set a fine example by taking his seat to welcome Jana Novotna and the Australian junior champion, Nicole Pratt (like Rod Laver and Roy Emerson, a player from North Queensland), for what was a pleasingly lively hors-d'oeuvre before the seeded Czechoslovakian picked up the pace from 3–3, for a 6–3, 6–0 victory.

For the rest of a day that produced 71 results, despite another couple of interruptions, there was action and excitement, mixed with nostalgia and more than a dash of British pride, almost everywhere one looked, as Wimbledon really felt like Wimbledon again.

Pride of place went once more to André Agassi, as he not only continued to play most of the right shots – and one crucially lucky one – but then also

said all the right things, and this hugely talented American earned a rousing reception from the Centre Court crowd on the completion of his 4–6, 6–1, 6–7, 7–5, 6–3 defeat of the resolute Grant Connell.

'I don't think I've ever enjoyed playing so much as I've done these last couple of days,' said the American, as he went into raptures about the whole experience, with an almost old-fashioned joy and respect that left those of us who have known him in less mature moments stunned by the happy transformation.

On wearing all-white, he said, 'It not only feels good but is a sign of respect for the tradition which is so obvious here.' On playing on grass, he described it as 'fun' and added, as you might expect from someone who lives in Las Vegas, 'It felt like a crap-shoot out there. You just kinda throw the dice and hope it rolls the right way.' And on Wimbledon in general? 'Before I came, I accepted one hundred per cent the traditions and all that Wimbledon offered sport. But showing up and getting on the Centre Court, I have to admit I fell for the excitement and classiness of it all. Wimbledon feels bigger than tennis. The fans are something you don't experience anywhere else in the world. They clap for the good shots and they don't cheer for errors.'

He also admitted that, despite a flood of lethal double-handed returns, he was lucky to survive for a second-round match against Yugoslavia's Goran Prpic. There was one moment in particular when the dice certainly rolled his way. It was in the fourth set, in which he had held three set points at 5–3 but had been caught at 5–5 by a series of loose shots, which continued as Connell gained the chance to break again and serve for the match. Agassi's first serve hardly reached the net. After the second he made a timid backhand response to Connell's return, but the ball hit the tape, bounced over the net and died.

'I think that net cord is the reason I'm playing in the next round and he's not. I got lucky and that's all there is to it,' he added, after turning the match his way with 12 of the next 13 points. Connell, who had seven times saved break points in that set before having his glimpse of victory, underlined his strength of character by saving more break points in the second, fourth and eighth games of the fifth before Agassi, double-faulting on his first match point, finished it with an ace. Connell, who had hit 17 aces, summed everything

Nicole Pratt feels the strain against Jana Novotna.

(Overleaf) Boris Becker (left), up, up and away against fellow German, Carl-Uwe Steeb, while Kelly Evernden (right) made it increasingly hard work for Ivan Lendl to beat him 6–2, 7–5, 7–6.

Sara Loosemore was kept on the run by former junior champion, Andrea Strnadova.

As eager as ever, Betsy Nagelson, 34 (top left), faced a 14-year age gap when she was beaten by Elena Brioukhovets of the USSR.

The pressure started to tell on Ivan Lendl from as early as his opening match against New Zealander, Kelly Evernden.

up perfectly when he said, 'I think he impressed a lot of people.' He did, in more ways than one.

At this stage of the tournament, Agassi was completely overshadowing others such as Boris Becker, who opened his bid to regain the title with a comfortable 6–4, 6–2, 6–4 defeat of fellow German Carl-Uwe Steeb. Agassi was also eclipsing his former room-mate Jim Courier – who completed a 6–4, 6–2, 7–6 victory over Frenchman Rodolphe Gilbert – and even Ivan Lendl, who made increasingly heavy weather of beating the New Zealander, Kelly Evernden, 6–2, 7–5, 7–6.

Few players upstage Jimmy Connors, however, not even at the age of 38, and over on Court 1 he was once more having the time of his life against an overawed Veli Paloheimo from Finland. It was only after a spectacular first week at the French Open that Connors, two matches away from playing his 100th singles at Wimbledon, persuaded NBC Television to let him out of the commentators' box and seek a wild card.

Like a handful of others, he had been waiting since Monday to play – rostered originally for Court 1, then Centre Court on Tuesday and Court 2 on Wednesday and Thursday, before finally making it on to Court 1 after all. If some of his shots lacked their former pace and power, it was nevertheless a virtuoso illustration of the Connors personality during the 97 minutes it took him to win 6–2, 6–0, 7–5. The crowd, with which he has always had such a special rapport, loved every moment, especially when he was feigning fatigue (or was it a double bluff?), or ordering his opponent with mock seriousness, 'Don't do that again' after a brilliant lob briefly questioned his authority early in the third set.

Tim Mayotte, 30, six times a quarter-finalist and once a semi-finalist, has also started to fall into the 'old-timer' category. Just before 8 pm he produced the only major upset of a memorable day by staging a brilliant recovery from two sets – and then four match points – down to repeat his 1989 defeat of ninth-seeded Michael Chang.

In what became a wonderfully thrilling struggle on Court 1, Mayotte, who had twice before won from two sets down at Wimbledon, saved two match points at 4–5 in the fourth set and two more in a tie-break he eventually won with a brilliant crosscourt backhand, on the way to his first success since February. Mayotte served 23 aces, two fewer than Goran Ivanisevic, who reached 25, which was a personal match record, while

Veli Paloheimo sums up the feelings of countless opponents of the swashbuckling Jimmy Connors over the years.

The stronger serving and powerful net play of a revitalized Tim Mayotte meant that not even a two sets lead was enough for Michael Chang.

Britain's Nick Brown celebrates his first singles win at Wimbledon, at the fourth attempt. He beat the American, Mark Keil, 6–4, 7–5, 6–1.

Aki Rahunen, the promising young Finnish player reaching for the sky, came down to earth with a straight sets defeat by Germany's Patrick Kuhnen.

A defiant enough stance from 11th seed, Emilio Sanchez, but it was not enough. Patrick McEnroe upset the rankings in straight sets.

finishing off Andrew Castle, 7–6, 7–6, 6–2.

Chang was not the only beaten seed – but he was the least expected. Hard on the heels of Andrei Cherkasov's departure the night before, there was a further reminder to the seeding committee that rankings are not always enough, let alone reliable, when Emilio Sanchez, predictably ill at ease whenever he left the baseline, was overpowered 6–3, 7–6, 6–1 by Patrick McEnroe.

The only seed to fall in the women's singles was the Italian Sandra Cecchini, similarly uncertain on grass, who was beaten 6–3, 3–6, 6–1 by Liz Smylie, an Australian clearly at home on the surface, as she was once more to prove in the doubles.

If there was any comeback on the day that beat Mayotte's, it was surely the 4–6, 4–6, 6–3, 6–3, 8–6 victory by Mark Petchey, the British number five, over the vastly more experienced Jim Pugh, even though most of the American's successes have come in doubles and he needed a wild card to compete in the singles, when Davis Cup duty prevented him from being in London in time for the qualifying.

What made Petchey's escape so remarkable was that, when he was 5–3 down in the third set and facing match point, Pugh hit a serve that both players initially thought was an ace. Certainly Petchey looked ready to move in and shake hands, until he realized that the linesman had called a fault. Meanwhile the cheers from Court 13 told him that Jeremy Bates, the British number one, had beaten José-Francisco Altur, a Spanish newcomer to the circuit and the last to be accepted straight into the draw on merit, 6–4, 6–4, 6–2. This undoubtedly helped inspire Petchey to fight back and go into a fifth set for the first time in his career.

Petchey, more that 200 places below Pugh in the world rankings, saved another match point at 4–5 and two break points one game later, before producing a brilliant sequence of winners to break Pugh to love in the 14th game. 'I suppose I'll give it a couple more years now,' he said after earning £5,880, the biggest pay-cheque of his career, just when he had been contemplating opting out of the tour after his 21st birthday, which was then only five weeks away.

A third British slot was booked in the second round when Nick Brown, ranked 591, beat Mark Keil, the little-known American who had beaten him in the qualifying rounds at Queen's Club before going on to beat Pete Sampras. 'It was nice to get a little bit of revenge,' commented Brown,

(Inset) Maya Kidowaki saved a match point on the way to beating Britain's Sarah Bentley.

'Peanut' Louie Harper ponders what to do next against Steffi Graf, who beat her 6–0, 6–1.

Fred Stolle (left) watches with another former Australian Davis Cup player, Owen Davidson, as his son, Sandon Stolle (right), eventually beats fellow countryman Mark Kratzmann (far right), in a marathon first-round match that ended 99 hours, 38 minutes after it should have started.

whose 6–4, 7–5, 6–1 victory took him into the second round for the first time in a career that started in 1982.

'I really wanted to enjoy myself because this might be my last Wimbledon,' said the 29-year-old Cheshire player, who had no inkling then of just how much more he was going to enjoy himself 24 hours later against Goran Ivanisevic.

The six British women players on duty on Day Five all lost, but Lincolnshire's Sarah Bentley had been leading Japan's Maya Kidowaki, 6–1, 5–4, 0–30, when drizzle forced them off Court 7. When they returned, under the full glare of the news cameras, she squandered the match point she quickly earned, with a weak backhand. Miss Kidowaki never looked back. She won 1–6, 7–5, 6–1. There was similar disappointment for Samantha Smith, who never played with the same control or conviction again after a delay when she was a set and 3–2 ahead of Nicole Provis, and the Australian recovered to win 3–6, 6–4, 6–2.

Any one of six matches due to have started on Day One might have claimed to be the longest match in Wimbledon history, but in the end the honour (if that is the right word for it) went to the clash between Sandon Stolle, 20 – son of three-

times former runner-up, Fred Stolle, in the mid 1960s – and fellow Australian, Mark Kratzmann. Stolle, who saved a match point in a fourth-set tie-break between two qualifiers, eventually won 6–7, 6–3, 6–7, 7–6, 6–4 at 3.58 pm, after no less than eight interruptions along the way, and 99 hours and 38 minutes after the match was originally listed to start.

Even so, three first-round men's singles matches due to have been played on Tuesday were still waiting to go on court. And although Steffi Graf had beaten 'Peanut' Louie Harper 6–0, 6–1 in the first and only women's second-round match so far finished, officials eventually decided that evening, after much agonized debate, that there was no alternative but to have play on the middle Sunday for the first time ever, in order to stand any chance of The Championships finishing on time.

It was, it seemed, a case of a desperate situation needing far more desperate measures than those already taken, such as reducing the men's doubles to the best of three sets, instead of the best of five, and transferring the juniors to Roehampton – although, in the event, this never happened.

D A Y

Saturday 29 June

It is not often that a British player, especially in the men's singles, worthily steals the headlines, if only for one day, at Wimbledon. But Nick Brown, in the twilight of a career that had never blossomed to its true potential, most certainly did on Day Six.

Amid enormous excitement for a packed and wildly patriotic crowd on Court 13, the Ealing-based British number two fought back after losing a tough first set to beat Goran Ivanisevic, the 10th seed and 1990 semi-finalist, 4–6, 6–3, 7–6, 6–3.

In world ranking terms, 11 against 591, it was one of the most lopsided results since rankings began in 1973. In British terms, it was the first time a home player had beaten a seed since John Lloyd eliminated Eliot Teltscher (whose love of grass is

Down but far from out. Nick Brown can afford to look pleased, despite the pose, on his way to upsetting 10th-seeded Goran Ivanisevic on Court 13.

Despite her growing passion for golf, Britain's Jo Durie is not pretending to be measuring a putt . . . just taking a breather after one of many tough points as she lost 6–3, 5–7, 6–3 to Holland's Manon Bollegraf.

(Overleaf) Perhaps it is as well that we do not know what Frenchman Thierry Champion (left) was saying after he lost a set to Britain's Chris Wilkinson. Studied concentration by Martina Navratilova (right) as she dismisses Britain's Amanda Grunfeld.

Pete Sampras, the US Open champion, shows how he felt after being 'licked' by fellow American, Derrick Rostagno, in the second round.

matched by Ted Heath's support for Margaret Thatcher), and was easily the best result since Lloyd beat Roscoe Tanner on Day One in 1977.

'I lost because I played badly. Brown played as well as he is capable and I did not,' said a sternly disappointed Ivanisevic. Not that such faint praise upset his victor, who arrived at and departed from The Championships each day as pillion passenger on his benefactor's motor cycle.

Playing, incidentally, on the only court that has the Union Jack fluttering alongside, Brown received a rapturous reception on his victory in 2 hours 23 minutes, which included a recovery from 1–4 in the third set and a devastating, diving volley to go four set points up at 6–2 in the tie-break.

Brown, who left the circuit in 1984 and was only lured back by the prospect of a Davis Cup debut in 1989, kept his nerve wonderfully after breaking in the fourth game of the fourth set and, although being punished for too short a serve on his first match point, his seventh ace clinched the moment of glory.

There were no such celebrations for the other British first-round winners. Mark Petchey was outclassed by Germany's Patrick Kuhnen, 6–2, 6–4, 6–3; Jeremy Bates put up a brave fight but lost in four sets to Tim Mayotte, who hit 19 aces; Jo

Diego Nargiso, the 1987 junior champion, at least had the satisfaction of taking a set from Michael Stich.

Durie saved two match points in the second set before losing to Manon Bollegraf; and Amanda Grunfeld had to be content with four games from Martina Navratilova on Court 1 after a sadly nervous start.

Brown's next opponent would be Thierry Champion, a Frenchman who, until this year, had not won a match in four Wimbledon visits, but who still managed to outlast, outpass and even outserve the 1987 champion, Pat Cash. The score was 7–5, 6–7, 4–6, 6–1, 12–10, ending what, for the rest of the world, was the most exciting match of the day, as well as producing the longest set.

The depression in Cash's mood later was a reflection of the way he played, especially in the final set, when he held two match points at 9–8. Champion saved the first with a mighty serve, but there were loud groans from Cash's sizeable army of supporters on Court 2 when he weakly netted a backhand on the second.

From then on Champion punished the increasingly lethargic Australian, especially for the double fault that cost him the decisive break four games later. Cash's attempt to lay some of the blame for his defeat on what he called the 'shocking' Court 2 was hardly justified. He simply lacked the pace, zest and flair required and was seldom sharp enough to volley effectively against an opponent who made only one voluntary volley in the whole of the fifth set.

Ivanisevic was not the only 'young pretender' for the men's singles crown who failed to last the first week. No sooner had the huge roar greeting Brown's triumph over Ivanisevic faded than Pete Sampras was leaving Court 3 after a 6–4, 3–6, 7–6, 6–4 defeat by fellow American Derrick Rostagno.

Since winning the US Open ten months earlier and then winning the inaugural Compaq Grand Slam Cup, adding around £2 million to his bank balance, Sampras, who yearns one day to be hailed as 'a right-handed Rod Laver', had struggled to find inspiration or form. Once again it was his serve, the key to his whole game, which let him down most against an opponent – and practice partner – who had underlined his own grass-court pedigree by beating John McEnroe in the first round a year earlier.

Jakob Hlasek, the 13th seed, was also beaten 6–3, 1–6, 7–5, 6–3, by Todd Woodbridge, 19, twice winner of the junior boys' doubles. Otherwise the big names, and also Michael Stich (soon to be a big name), progressed without too many distractions.

54

Stich dropped a third-set tie-break to Diego Nargiso before winning 6–3, 6–4, 6–7, 6–2, but as the Italian is a former winner of the junior boys' title, such things can happen. For the most part, the German confirmed the rating he had won from his impressive first-round defeat of Dan Goldie, and demonstrated that he had a better chance than most of upsetting higher-ranked, more experienced rivals when the time came.

Boris Becker, who perhaps should have made more of an impact at the time, was still not fully into his attacking style, labouring more than he would have liked for a 7–6, 7–5, 7–5 defeat of Sweden's Bjorn Borg lookalike, Peter Lundgren. But no such worries at that stage for Stefan Edberg. He beat David Pate 6–2, 6–2, 6–3 and announced, 'As we're behind schedule, it's good to be able to conserve energy.'

Meanwhile André Agassi's new courtship with Wimbledon advanced a step further, when he earned another standing ovation – this time on Court 1 – for his 7–6, 3–6, 6–4, 6–2 defeat of Goran Prpic. 'I feel as if I'm a qualifier, having the best tournament of his life,' said Agassi who, after an occasionally uncertain start, took charge from the moment he struck two backhand returns with enormous speed and power to break his stylish opponent in the 10th game of the third set.

On the first point of the fourth set, Prpic, again beaten by the angle and pace of the American's return, fell and sat forlornly on the grass. For a moment one wondered whether it was more serious than it looked, for Prpic has to wear a full-length leg brace, after major knee surgery, to protect his career. In fact, the fall caused no more than damaged pride that he could no longer curb the flow of winning passing shots from Agassi, who came round the net to help his rival back to his feet.

While Agassi was providing another perfect example of how to win friends and influence people, John McEnroe was going through an all too familiar routine of keeping himself and the officials on tenterhooks for more than three hours, before overcoming Sandon Stolle on the Centre Court.

The decisive fourth-set tie-break, which Sandon's proud father was describing to television viewers back home in Australia, typified the unevenness of McEnroe's performance and the bravery of Stolle's gritty resistance. From 0–3, after Stolle, 20, a tall newcomer and qualifier, had hit

Brenda Schultz, from Holland, created the biggest first-week upset in the ladies' singles by knocking out sixth-seeded Jana Novotna in the second round.

John McEnroe, who took four sets to beat qualifier, Sandon Stolle, no longer has quite the same mystical power over his racket.

55

Andrea Strnadova scurries towards a 6–1, 6–3 defeat of Carrie Cunningham.

two superb forehand winners, McEnroe moved to 5–3 with a glorious mixture of powered and subtle shots. Yet at 5–4 he netted the simplest of forehands and, on his first match point, was unable to prevent Stolle, who had saved 13 break points in the first two sets, from escaping again with a solid forehand volley.

Indeed, with Stolle hitting another couple of service winners, McEnroe had to save a set point in similar fashion before reaching match point for a second time with an ace, and taking it with a classic forehand service return.

Between some vintage points, however, there were some vintage McEnroe complaints. From as early on as the eighth game he was muttering darkly about the line judge who, he complained, 'has been bugging me for 13 years'. More than once he demanded of the umpire, 'How far does it have to be out before you over-rule?' It was quite like old times, especially with Jimmy Connors also romping to what was surely an embarrassing 6–3, 6–2, 6–3 defeat for fellow American, Aaron Krickstein, 15 years Connors' junior.

It was certainly a fitting way for Connors to celebrate his century of singles matches at Wimbledon, although the 1974 and 1982 champion was not unduly impressed. 'Just business as usual,' he said. 'If you think about things like that it is added pressure, and I don't need that at this time.' With that, he headed for the NBC television studio behind Court 14, saying, 'I've finished my tennis for the day. Now I'm going to work.'

The first Saturday also produced other shocks, with two more seeds losing in the women's doubles and, even more surprisingly, the holders, Rick Leach and Jim Pugh, being beaten 6–3, 6–4 in the opening defence of their men's doubles title by what might have seemed the unlikely combination of Goran Ivanisevic and John McEnroe.

Brenda Schultz, the powerfully built, tall blonde from Holland, who won the junior girls' title in 1988 (when she was also ranked number one among her country's skiers) caused the principal upset in the women's singles with her 6–4, 7–6, 6–4 defeat of the sixth seed, Jana Novotna.

Miss Schultz won with a flurry of hard serving and volleying against an opponent not renowned for her mental strength under pressure, although the way Miss Novotna saved three match points amid a teasing wind at 3–5 in the final set suggested that the problem is one she is well capable of overcoming in the future.

Although Miss Novotna had served for the match at 6–5 in the second set and had led 2–0 in the third, her confidence was undermined by the severity and consistency of Miss Schultz's returns, especially off the backhand. And later Linda Harvey-Wild, who had made great strides in the months leading up to Wimbledon, achieved what many fellow players had forecast by beating Natalia Zvereva, the 12th seed, 6–4, 6–1.

Youngsters Jennifer Capriati and Anke Huber made impressive progress, while there were other second-round wins for Arantxa Sanchez Vicario, once she woke up from trailing 0–3 to Amanda Coetzer; for Zina Garrison, last year's runner-up, warning that 'people are again underestimating me'; and for Gabriela Sabatini, who played reasonably well for her 6–4, 6–2 victory over Karine Quentrec, the diminutive French player ranked only 71 in the world, but who admitted honestly and prophetically, as it turned out, that 'To win, I'm going to have to start better in matches and improve my serve.'

One of many two-handed backhands as Karine Quentrec went down against Gabriela Sabatini.

Middle Sunday

Sunday 30 June

Wimbledon had never known a day like it. It was the day when the world's most famous tennis garden party became a joyful carnival – a day which no one lucky enough to have been there, in whatever capacity, will ever forget.

When the gates opened only about 13,000 people were estimated to be queuing for this first middle-Sunday occasion – an emergency operation to try and catch up on the first week's backlog of matches. It was first come, first served, at a bargain price of £10 a head for seats on Centre Court and Court 1 and a mere £5 to watch play on the other 16 courts.

John Curry (far right), Chairman of The All England Club, and Ian King, President of The Lawn Tennis Association, led the 'Wimbledon wave' from the Royal Box on memorable 'Middle Sunday'. Jean Borotra and Kitty Godfree, former champions, had clearly never seen anything like it.

Ivan Lendl in full serving flow.

(Overleaf) 'You cannot be serious. That ball was a foot out,' John McEnroe (left) insists. He lost the argument but still beat Jean Fleurian of France, 6–2, 7–6, 6–1. Stefan Edberg (right) moved impressively through to the last 16 by dropping only six games against Christo Van Rensburg.

Lori McNeil, beaten 6–2, 6–4 by Arantxa Sanchez Vicario.

Jennifer Capriati had more problems than some had expected against Germany's Wiltrud Probst.

Dire warnings urging people not to travel from afar – in case they could not get in – another uninviting weather forecast and the inevitable, but sensible, late notice of the operation made sure that neither Wimbledon nor the local community was overwhelmed. Yet by the end of the day, as thousands more Londoners joined the die-hards, many of whom had camped outside overnight, no fewer than 24,894 had passed through the turnstiles. And what a time they had!

They cheered almost everyone and everything, from startled golfers who found their successful putts being greeted by great roars from those in the queues alongside the course, to the ground staff, the ball boys and girls and, of course, every player. The one exception: the umpire and linesmen. For them there were boos, though only in fun.

Scott and Jan Barribal from Honiton, one of the earliest to claim seats on the Centre Court, typified

the youthfulness, exuberance and dedication of the occasion. Both persistent overnight queuers, who regret the passing of the Centre Court standing enclosure, they met for the first time in the queue in 1985 and were married in 1989. They had driven up from Devon on the Friday, queued all night to spend Saturday watching matches, mostly on Court 1, and then immediately joined the queue again for 'Super Sunday'. 'It's like winning the Pools,' Scott said.

Long before Gabriela Sabatini and Andrea Strnadova, winner of the junior singles title in the two previous years, appeared to a prolonged standing ovation, the first of endless Mexican – sorry, 'Wimbledon' – waves had started. Even the Royal Box, later to be filled for the day with great players from the past, joined in.

In mid-afternoon, when rain briefly threatened to spoil the party, John Barrett, for BBC TV, introduced many of the former players to the crowd. It responded with renewed delight and with no hint of a generation gap, as the wonderful reception for

95-year-old Kitty Godfree and 92-year-old Jean Borotra, the 'Bounding Basque' (who was still playing doubles at Wimbledon when he was 65), emotionally illustrated.

During the knock-ups, the first reaction of the crowd was to cheer every time the ball was hit. Then they began counting each shot. Judging by what they were wearing, many of the spectators were also soccer fans, but any fears that soccer habits might filter through to Wimbledon were groundless.

The moment the umpire called 'play' you could have heard a pin drop. After her 6–1, 6–3 victory, in a match in which the Czechoslovakian seemed overawed by the occasion and did not do herself justice, Miss Sabatini described the whole experience as 'great fun. I couldn't stop laughing during the warm-up.' Martina Navratilova, both before and after her comfortable 6–2, 6–2 defeat of Laura Garrone on Court 2, was so intrigued by the noise on Centre Court that she could not resist taking a look for herself. 'It was awesome,' she said.

Maria Strandlund from Sweden could not stop Zina Garrison reaching the fourth round.

'Oops, I shouldn't have done that,' Arantxa Sanchez Vicario (top left) seems to be saying . . . but no matter. She still beat Lori McNeil.

'I couldn't help thinking: Gabby, you're the lucky one to be out there.'

Perhaps the most amazing welcome was reserved for Jimmy Connors. Long before he appeared, to face Derrick Rostagno in a third-round match, they were chanting, 'Jim-mee, Jim-mee.' And their devotion remained undiminished, even though this day – which Christopher Gorringe, The All England Club's Chief Executive, likened to 'The Last Night of the Proms' – may also turn out to have been 'Jimmy's last stand'.

Connors, who appeared to damage an ankle when chasing a drop volley on the first point of the tie-break, was beaten 7–6, 6–1, 6–4, although not without an appropriate cavalier finish when he returned, refreshed after an hour's rain delay, to save four match points before bowing out. 'I just wish it had been like that for the last twenty years. It was a great atmosphere,' said the American who, when he thinks in those terms, probably now regrets that he opted out of the last similarly memorable and historical Centre Court day – the parade of former champions to celebrate the Centenary of The Championships in 1977.

For all the emotion when Connors was on court, most of the real drama came on the outside courts. Ivan Lendl, in particular, looked even more worried than usual, when he was two sets down and 4–4 in the third set of a marvellous 3 hour 18 minute contest against the relatively inexperienced American Malivai Washington, on Court 2.

By that time Washington, a sturdy hitter with a similar physique, had superbly saved four crucial break points in four different games. Inevitably the question being asked was, 'Will Court 2, on which so many other high-flying dreams had floundered in the past, claim another victim?'

Lendl, however, was never bothered by such thoughts. He exorcized the idea of a Court 2 ghost by fighting back to win 4–6, 2–6, 6–4, 6–4, 7–5, claiming his 200th singles victory in the four Grand Slam tournaments. 'I think the Court 2 issue is just a myth,' he said, although he did admit, 'There was a remote possibility in my mind that I could have lost.' It was just as Washington was finding it increasingly difficult to sustain his early pace and consistency that Lendl's control returned, in time to refurbish his whole game.

What ultimately undermined the modestly ranked Washington (68) was that his serve, which he had employed so boldly and effectively to save

three of the break points against him, let him down. 'I think I became a bit nervous,' he said, after double-faulting to lose the third set and repeating the error to go 30–40 down in the fifth, as Lendl broke back decisively to 4–4 with an explosive crosscourt forehand winner. Yet another double fault offered Lendl a match point in the 10th game. Washington survived with a service winner, but two games later Lendl finished in full cry, first by chasing faster and more eagerly than in earlier sets to hit a spectacular pass, and then with a match-winning service return.

By contrast Stefan Edberg, the top seed, once again sailed through to the last 16 without dropping a set. Although he went through one period of lost concentration, he generally looked in splendid form as he beat Christo Van Rensburg 6–1, 6–3, 6–2. Also advancing unobtrusively but effectively to the fourth round were Jim Courier, who dropped only four games against French qualifier Arnaud Boetsch; Michael Stich, whose heavy serving just kept him ahead in four sets against Omar Camporese; and John McEnroe, although he could not resist another couple of verbal outbursts

against Australian umpire Richard Ings, who also had to give him a warning for racket abuse during a 6–2, 7–6, 6–1 win against Jean Fleurian.

After his match, McEnroe nipped out to see the final stages of his brother Patrick's contest with Jacco Eltingh, one of a record five Dutch players who made it into the men's singles draw. The former champion did not quite time it as well as he might have liked. He missed the two match points that Patrick held, but not the second match point that Eltingh took for a 7–6, 2–6, 1–6, 6–4, 12–10 triumph.

Initially some of the outside courts attracted only a handful of spectators, but that was certainly not true on Court 13, where Nick Brown, the overnight domestic hero, was attempting to become the first British player to reach the fourth round of the men's singles since Buster Mottram in 1982. The atmosphere was fantastic, but although Brown often served and rallied valiantly, he eventually had to yield to the more consistent passing power of the Frenchman, Thierry Champion.

The world number 90 somehow always looked

likely to beat the world number 591, as he should have done, but not before 29-year-old Brown had thrilled his supporters by taking control at the net as often as he could. An outbreak of cramp in the 11th game of the third set added to the pressure Brown was already under from double-faulting twice near the end of the first-set tie-break. Champion won 7–6, 1–6, 7–5, 6–3.

All 12 of the seeds in the women's singles who had survived thus far won again and, in all honesty, without too much concern, with only three of them being extended to a third set. Even so, Yayuk Basuki, a slightly built newcomer from Indonesia, confirmed the attractive impression she had made earlier, despite losing 6–2, 6–3 to Steffi Graf. And, for a while, Jennifer Capriati found herself in mostly self-inflicted trouble against fellow German Wiltrud Probst. 'I just can't concentrate properly, I don't know why. It's something I have to work on,' Miss Capriati confessed.

She also knew it was matter of some urgency. Her next opponent would be Brenda Schultz, who was confident enough after her previous day's victory over Jana Novotna to save two match points while squeezing past Elena Brioukhovets of the Soviet Union, 5–7, 6–4, 7–5.

Overall, Wimbledon's 'Middle Sunday' was one of those magical occasions that you never really wanted to end, not least because reality told you it can probably never be repeated – certainly not in the foreseeable future. On a regular basis the numbers likely to want to be invited would render it frighteningly impracticable.

Many of those who had relished the day's 'Open House' lingered long after the last ball had been hit – some hoping to find one of the 10,000 special programmes that were already precious souvenirs, changing hands at five times their £1 face value.

For many, the finest part of a day that was summed up by Club Chairman John Curry, when he said, 'What noise, what enthusiasm, what discipline and what happiness', came with the bonus mixed doubles match on Centre Court late in the evening.

Steffi Graf, looking happier and more relaxed on court than anyone could remember, partnered Henri Leconte, the perfect entertainer for the occasion, in a 6–1, 6–2 defeat of Charles Beckman and 'Peanut' Louie Harper, in a match that left even the losers feeling radiant at the end. The smiles on everyone's faces, throughout the day, said it all.

Ivan Lendl obliges an autograph hunter – and the photographers – after surviving a gruelling contest on Court 2 against Malivai Washington.

Zina Garrison (left) demonstrates the determination that carried her to the final a year earlier.

D A Y

7

Monday 1 July

Sadly for Ivan Lendl, and the many spectators who would have been equally delighted to see him win the only major tournament title that still eludes him, Wimbledon returned to normal in more ways than one for Day Seven, on the second Monday. In particular, there was an all too familiar end – albeit earlier than usual – to the 12th chapter of what has become the former world champion's magnificent obsession.

As each successive year goes by, it becomes that much more difficult for Lendl, now 31, to win what might be regarded as 'generation games', and so it proved against David Wheaton, nine years his junior. Lendl's 6–3, 3–6, 7–6, 6–3 defeat was his earliest in any Grand Slam tournament since he was beaten in the summer of 1981 in the first round at Wimbledon by the unseeded Australian, Charlie Fancutt.

Disappointing as the match must have been for the Connecticut-based Czechoslovakian – who had taken on Chris Lewis, the 1983 runner-up, earlier in the year, to supplement the guidance he continues to receive for major events from coach Tony Roche – it cannot have come as the greatest surprise.

These days Lendl has unmistakably lost some of the cutting edge from his serve and, just as damagingly, from his returns. And no sooner had he arrived in Europe in May than he needed surgery for the removal of scar tissue deep inside the palm of his racket hand. That, and his early defeat at Queen's Club, left Lendl ominously short of serious match play with which to combat the extra vigour and service power of his opponent. Wheaton, a 6 ft 4 in, supremely confident serve and volleyer, was happy to keep producing performances that reminded everyone that he should have been seeded.

Wheaton's combination of 16 aces, even more service winners and a whole host of blistering returns, especially off the backhand, was just too much for Lendl to cope with, less than 24 hours after his escape against Malivai Washington. Lendl had his chances. In fact, the chilling statistic in this respect was that Lendl won only two of the 14 break points he had on Wheaton's serve, whereas he survived only three of the eight against him.

'He took advantage of his break points, whereas I didn't take advantage of mine,' said Lendl, who could have been forgiven if his mind was occasionally wandering across the Atlantic to his home, where wife Samantha had returned a few days earlier to await the birth of their twins. Lendl's last realistic chance vanished during the tie-break of the third set, after he had earlier recovered from Wheaton's 4–1 lead in the set itself. He had a set point at 6–5 in the tie-break but Wheaton, swiftly in behind his serve, coolly put away the volley.

Perhaps Boris Becker, who went through another of his worrying lapses of concentration, which cost him a set before he beat Andrei Olhovskiy 6–1, 6–4, 3–6, 6–3, summed up Lendl's predicament best of all when he said, 'He's fit. That's not the problem. But there are more and more good players now than there used to be, and with age it doesn't get any easier. It's more in your mind than in your body.'

Wheaton's success, more than adequate compensation for a player who had been beaten in the first round of his first four tournaments in 1991, meant that there would be eight unseeded players among the last 16. Among the others who joined the list on this day was Christian Bergstrom, a quarter-finalist in 1990, who upset an often grumpy Brad Gilbert on Court 4 to win 6–3, 6–2, 3–6, 6–3.

David Wheaton celebrates one of his frequent powerful winners, which gave Ivan Lendl his earliest Wimbledon defeat since 1981.

Jan Gunnarsson became one of three Swedish players in the last 16 with his victory over Todd Woodbridge.

Boris Becker shows what he thinks of himself for letting slip the third set against Andrei Olhovskiy on Court 1.

When he failed to break Bergstrom at 2–2 in the second set, the American, seeded 15, hurled his racket into the net. When he was broken to trail 2–4, he swept a ball high out over the adjoining main concourse. Those on the members' balcony ducked as it buried itself into the ivy above them. The obligatory code violation followed.

Other unseeded players who joined Thierry Champion, Derrick Rostagno and Alexander Volkov, who were already there, were Jacco Eltingh, playing in his first year of Grand Slam tournaments; Jan Gunnarsson, who carried too much weight of shot for Todd Woodbridge; and the veteran Tim Mayotte. He maintained his enjoyable, as well as rewarding, renaissance with a 3–6, 6–2, 7–6, 6–4 defeat of Germany's Patrick Kuhnen who, having broken to lead 6–5 in the third set, immediately lost his own service and then the tie-break.

Mayotte's next opponent would be Guy Forget, the seventh seed, who had been outwitted and often outhit in the first two sets by fellow Frenchman, Henri Leconte, making nonsense of his world ranking 85 places below his Davis Cup doubles partner. Then suddenly, according to Leconte, who had undergone two occasions of back surgery in the previous two years, 'There was a lock in my back and it got worse and worse.' He lost the third set and was 1–4 down in the fourth when he knew he could take no more, although prompt work by his trainer, Jerome Bianchi, the former French Rugby Union international, who manipulated the dislodged vertebrae back into place, meant that he would still be able to play another round of mixed doubles with Steffi Graf the following day.

There was an injury too on Court 1, during André Agassi's 7–6, 6–3, 7–6 defeat of another of those promising Dutchmen, Richard Krajicek, only in this instance it involved Natasha Tunks from Putney Vale, one of the wonderfully efficient ball girls who, for the first time, outnumbered the ball boys. Natasha slipped and sprained her ankle and then fainted. Both players joined officials in comforting her, before carrying her to the first-aid room, much to the delight of the Fleet Street photographers. Fortunately the injury was not serious, and she was back on duty before the end of the week.

The injury happened just when Krajicek, 19 and 6 ft 3 in with a serve and reach in keeping with such details, was seriously threatening to take the

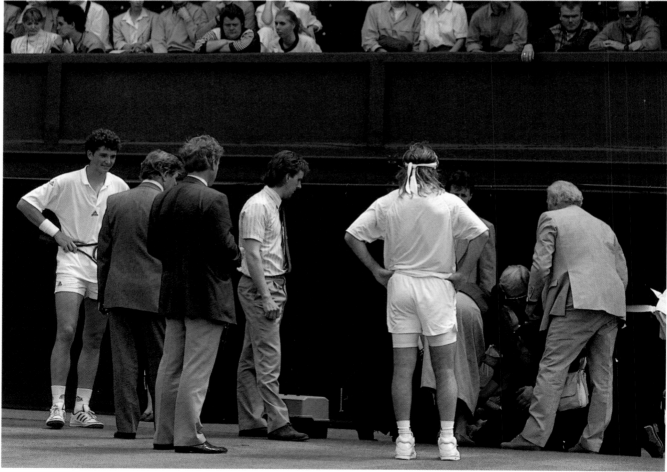

André Agassi played two of his five matches on Court 1 and joined others, including his opponent, Richard Krajicek, in making sure ball girl Natasha Tunks was not badly injured after twisting her ankle.

(Above) André and his sunglasses. He took them off once the sun appeared.

(Overleaf) Another convincing day at the office for Martina Navratilova as she beat Catarina Lindqvist, 6–1, 6–3.

Anke Huber in profile as she waits to receive serve from Zina Garrison.

Arantxa Sanchez Vicario (right) had to save four set points in the first set before going on to beat Anne Minter 7–5, 3–6, 6–1.

initiative in the second set. At 2–2, Agassi was 0–40 down but, just as he had lifted his game when two points from losing the first set, he did so again when they resumed after a five-minute delay, although Krajicek did not help himself by staying back instead of continuing to try and take charge at the net.

The injury to the ball girl had not been the only diversion. For the first three games, even though it was dark and overcast with drizzle in the air all the time, Agassi wore spectacular yellow-rimmed ski-style sunglasses. Apparently aghast that anyone should think it was another commercial gimmick, even though he frequently dropped the manufacturer's name into the conversation, he said, 'They're similar to what skiers use when it's cloudy, and I've been practising with them a lot. Once the sun comes out I don't need them.'

'Tell that to the marines,' a voice from the back of the interview room was heard to say.

On the women's front, it was another relatively straightforward day in terms of results, though many of the individual performances were disappointing. Gabriela Sabatini, for instance, admitted that she was still playing too negatively to stand a credible chance of winning the title. 'I know I'm going to have to serve and volley a whole lot more in the remaining matches,' she said after a

pedestrian 7–6, 6–3 defeat of the French player Nathalie Tauziat.

A day earlier, when Miss Sabatini had opened the Centre Court programme, she received a thunderous welcome from a nearly full stadium, complete with wolf whistles. This time there was just a ripple of polite applause from about 2,000 when the match began at 11.45 am, 45 minutes later than planned because of another shower. Perhaps that had some bearing on the mediocre nature of the first set before more rain again sent the players scurrying for cover early in the tie-break.

It was not until midway through the second set that Miss Sabatini started to hit out with any freedom. Zina Garrison, on Court 14, only took charge of a strange match with the young German, Anke Huber, in the third set, when she needed just 19 minutes to complete a 4–6, 6–3, 6–0 victory. Martina Navratilova did not look entirely comfortable either against Catarina Lindqvist, but dismissed such impertinent suggestions. 'I felt great out there,' she retorted after a 6–1, 6–3 win in a record 112th singles match, one more than Chris Evert and two more than her coach Billie Jean King.

Four more seeds were beaten but, with the exception of Katerina Maleeva, simply by higher seeds. Miss Maleeva is happiest on clay, so her 3–6,

6–2, 6–3 defeat by Laura Gildemeister, who is much more at home on faster surfaces, was not entirely surprising.

Arantxa Sanchez Vicario made countless unforced errors, and it was only after saving four set points at 4–5 in the first set, when Australia's Anne Minter became tentative, that she went on to a 7–5, 3–6, 6–1 victory. Meanwhile Mary Joe Fernandez had to work hard in the second set for her 6–0, 7–5 win against Austria's Judith Wiesner.

The one player who could feel content with her day's work was Jennifer Capriati. She was in trouble for a while against Brenda Schultz, the player with the hardest and fastest serve (110 miles per hour) in women's tennis, but Miss Schultz also double-faulted too often and, having broken in the first game of the third set, Miss Capriati swept on with an impressive variety of drives and lobs from the baseline, to win 3–6, 6–1, 6–1.

As for the main doubles news of the day, a new face with a familiar name stole the honours. Doug Flach, 20, brother of former doubles champion Ken, volleyed brilliantly as he and Jim Courier excitingly upset Goran Ivanisevic and John McEnroe, after their first-round defeat of the holders, 3–6, 7–6, 6–4.

D A Y

Tuesday 2 July

Stefan Edberg, a defending champion seemingly at the peak of his career, gave a virtuoso display against John McEnroe, a former champion living on memories, before more rain returned to provide further scheduling headaches on a day when neither the women's quarter-finals nor the fourth-round matches in the men's singles was completed.

It was also a day when Michael Stich benefited from a lucky net cord, which he may well look back upon as the most crucial point in the transformation of his career; when The All England Club claimed another success in their clampdown on ticket touts; and when, by nightfall, two major issues remained in suspense.

One was whether the rain, which had started at 3.38 pm and remained frustratingly for the rest of the day, would provide Martina Navratilova with the opportunity to maintain the recovery she had seemingly just started, after losing the first set to Jennifer Capriati.

The other was how Wimbledon officials would react to the barrage of abuse which McEnroe had apparently directed at a linesman towards the end of his 7–5, 6–1, 6–4 defeat by Edberg, once they had viewed the tape that Independent Television News had censored with several bleeps before putting on the air.

McEnroe, still clinging fondly to the belief that 'hope springs eternal' in his quest to add to the last of the three Wimbledon titles he won seven years

'Where shall I put my next winner?' ponders Stefan Edberg against John McEnroe (right), who loves the last word, even when he cannot win the last point.

earlier, fell out twice during the match with different officials on the same line. On both occasions he insisted that serves from Edberg were 'like a foot out'.

Whatever case he may have had on the first occasion, when he certainly had the sympathy of the crowd, on the second the ball clearly found the side of the line, and McEnroe was lucky that few others, apart from a linesman too stunned to react quickly enough, apparently heard him at the time; otherwise there could have been swift, instant punishment.

It was a pity, because the incident overshadowed a most prosperous display from Edberg, as, just like David Wheaton against Ivan Lendl the day before, he exploited the diminishing pace and penetration of his opponent's once-classic form. It showed as early as the first game when Edberg hit the sort of return to the American's feet which, at his best, in 1983–4, McEnroe would have flicked back as an exquisite half-volley or volley winner. No longer.

It showed too in McEnroe's second serves which, particularly in the second and third sets, the top seed returned with a vengeance. The first set lasted 66 minutes, but as the McEnroe batteries started to run low, the next two lasted only an hour. Edberg took the second set in a mere 22 minutes. Indeed, after two tight games at the start of the set, he took 22 of the next 24 points, and then from 0–3 in the third set there was a renewed Swedish sprint, as he took 20 of the next 25 points.

Despite McEnroe's promise, repeated more than once during the fortnight, that he really had learned how to respond with equanimity to line-calls that he felt were wrong, the supportive evidence was disappointingly thin. The only thing that seemed to have changed was the brightness of the spark in his tennis.

Edberg had to wait overnight to see if Thierry Champion could collect the extra six points he needed – from 4–1 up in the fifth set against Derrick Rostagno, when the rain came – to be his next challenger. Meanwhile Jim Courier, David

One of several lucky escapes for Michael Stich against Alexander Volkov.

Wheaton and Michael Stich all progressed, but the match of Guy Forget versus Tim Mayotte remained in the balance, although in the Frenchman's favour. Boris Becker and André Agassi were left kicking their heels in the dressing rooms. The rain came before they even got on court.

Although, with more time to think about it, Jim Courier might have reconsidered his belief that he is another Ivan Lendl on grass (because he is not a natural player on the surface, rather than because he does not believe he will ever become Wimbledon champion), he could be pleased by the fact that his solid 6–3, 6–4, 6–2 defeat of Karel Novacek made him a quarter-finalist at only his third attempt.

Winning in five sets against Jim Grabb in the second round had been something of a break-through for Courier, who is seldom to be seen on court without a baseball cap. He reflected satisfactorily, 'I think my transition to the net game has been a lot quicker and easier than I thought it would be.'

Jennifer Capriati was quickly into the swing of things as she set about upsetting Martina Navratilova.

80

Courier, still basking in the glow of beating Agassi in the French Open final to become champion a month earlier, would next meet his semi-final victim in that tournament, Michael Stich. Stich eventually beat Alexander Volkov 4–6, 6–3, 7–5, 1–6, 7–5 in a match during which the quality was as topsy-turvy as its progress.

When Volkov broke in the first game of the final set, and held that advantage until he served for the match at 5–4, it looked as if the German's hopes had ended. In fact, Volkov was two points from victory at 30–30 when he pulled Stich wide with a volley, and he could only look on in disbelief as the German somehow managed to reach out and get a backhand touch to the ball. It still looked to be going out, until it clipped the net cord and bounced over the Soviet player's outstretched racket.

Instead of being at match point, Volkov was now a break point down. Stich, taking full advantage of the situation, went on to break and take the next two games for victory. 'That net cord was the turning point,' he said afterwards. 'I think it is one of the most important points I have ever played.' Just how important, he could not possibly have guessed at the time. Perhaps Boris Becker did. After all, it was so reminiscent of the match point he saved in similar fashion against Derrick Rostagno in the second round of the US Open in 1989 ... when he went on to win the title.

Meanwhile, David Wheaton, waiting for Agassi or Jacco Eltingh, cruised into the quarter-finals with an emphatic 6–4, 6–3, 6–1 defeat of Jan Gunnarsson.

Steffi Graf was also all smiles. She took 66 minutes to avenge her semi-final defeat by Zina Garrison a year earlier, and for much of the 25-minute opening set she produced her most confident tennis against a quality opponent, on the way to a 6–1, 6–3 triumph. 'The way I started and the way I generally played made me feel really good,' said the German, emerging from 18 months of strains and stresses on and off the court. She looked suitably brisk and businesslike in maintaining her record of not having conceded more than four games in any of her first five matches.

For her part, Mary Joe Fernandez produced one of her best grass-court displays to give Miss Graf a further boost by removing Arantxa Sanchez Vicario – the Spaniard who had inflicted the worst physical and psychological defeat of Graf's career four weeks earlier in Paris. Miss Fernandez, the

Mary Joe Fernandez cast an anxious eye at the skies, hoping the rain would keep off long enough for her to complete her solid victory over Arantxa Sanchez Vicario (far right), who was asking herself, 'How could I have played such a stupid shot?'

Laura Gildemeister (right) found it hard to upset Gabriela Sabatini's rhythm.

fifth seed, beat Miss Sanchez Vicario, the fourth seed, with a run of four games from 2–2 in the first set. Although the American was broken when she served for victory at 5–3 in the second set, she quickly reasserted her authority with fine service returns to take it 7–5.

The first genuine drama of the women's Championship, however, was unfolding on Centre Court, where Miss Capriati had made it abundantly clear from the outset that she would not be intimidated by an opponent who had been a finalist 11 times and the champion nine times in 19 years.

Taking the ball cleanly and early, she had chances to break Miss Navratilova in both the second and sixth games, before doing so in the eighth, to make it 5–3 with a sparkling crosscourt backhand. Navratilova was stunned. Two double faults in that game had suggested panic beneath an outwardly calm surface. She responded magnificently, attacking every serve by Miss Capriati,

to break back to love. But the problem was still her own serve. At 40–15 she looked secure, but the youngster reached deuce with two brilliant returns. A miscued backhand made it set point, and a look of disbelief crossed the defending champion's face as a stinging serve, which she seemed to believe might have been a fault, was drummed straight back past her. Though Miss Navratilova immediately broke for 2–0 in the second set, she had much to ponder over with coach Craig Kardon as she sat later in the Centre Court, watching it rain on a scoreboard that showed her just 3–2 ahead. Not least for her to ponder over were the four points she held for 4–1, before the youngster held a marathon fifth game.

D A Y

Wednesday 3 July

Overnight there had been more torrential rain, more than an inch apparently, and but for the vigilance of one of the night-watchmen who spotted water seeping under the court cover from a blocked drain, Court 2 could have been put out of action by flooding.

Yet by mid-morning there was bright, warm sunshine, most of the outside courts were only half an hour late being made available for play, and it was all systems go for a day in which no less than 102 matches were played – more than double the total for the first four days, and only 14 less than the modern documented record for any day, that of 116 in 1980.

It was just as well. There was much unfinished business needing attention, such as the repercussions of John McEnroe's outburst. But by the time the announcement was made of his fine of 10,000 US dollars – the maximum possible, and the highest ever imposed at Wimbledon – for what was officially described as 'flagrant verbal abuse', other events had certainly relegated the issue in terms of priority.

The enduring memory from Day Nine will be how Martina Navratilova, The Queen of the Centre Court, was despatched summarily and sometimes ruthlessly by a teenage princess with a smile as bright and natural as most of her winners.

In just 27 minutes, after they resumed from the overnight disruption, with Miss Navratilova a set down but serving at 3–2 in the second, Miss Capriati went on to a remarkably poised 6–4, 7–5 victory. This not only made her, at 15 years, 96 days, the youngest semi-finalist in the history of The Championships, but suggested that even Lottie Dod's record as the youngest champion (15 years 287 days) in 1887 might be in peril.

After some uncertain displays earlier in the year and, indeed, in earlier rounds at Wimbledon, which prompted the belief that Miss Capriati was finding life tougher on the circuit the second time around than the first, the young American responded with another performance which tended to confirm that she will produce her best on the biggest occasion.

Certainly, she appeared totally uninhibited by the surroundings, this particular occasion or the reputation of her opponent. On the very first point after they resumed she hit the sort of scorching service return that must have sown seeds of doubt – and fear – in Miss Navratilova's mind. In the past the champion, at least a semi-finalist every year since 1977, had steadfastly rejected such fallibility. This time she almost admitted it.

As the oldest competitor against the youngest ruefully admitted, after failing to sustain the service break she had carried over from Tuesday night, 'She was able to handle her serve a lot better than I did.' Miss Capriati had no nerves. Miss Navratilova, with those four lost break points at 3–1 the night before adding to the pain, again failed to break through when her young rival was 0–40 at 2–4. She added, 'Whenever I didn't get my first serve in, I was on my heels. That certainly didn't help my second serve.'

'I was so afraid of her returns that I ended up double-faulting,' she said in explanation of the calamitous final point. 'It was a total sin, but that's the way it goes.' It was, in fact, the second double fault of the game. The first, immediately after Miss Capriati had struck an unnerving forehand return winner, made it 0–30. At 15–40 Miss Navratilova saved two match points, the first with a classic serve and volley, the other when Miss Capriati went for a backhand pass, which fell back off the tape.

Undeterred, Miss Capriati hit an even more audacious backhand swinging winner to make it

Me and my shadow. Gabriela Sabatini proves that the sun did eventually shine on Wimbledon '91.

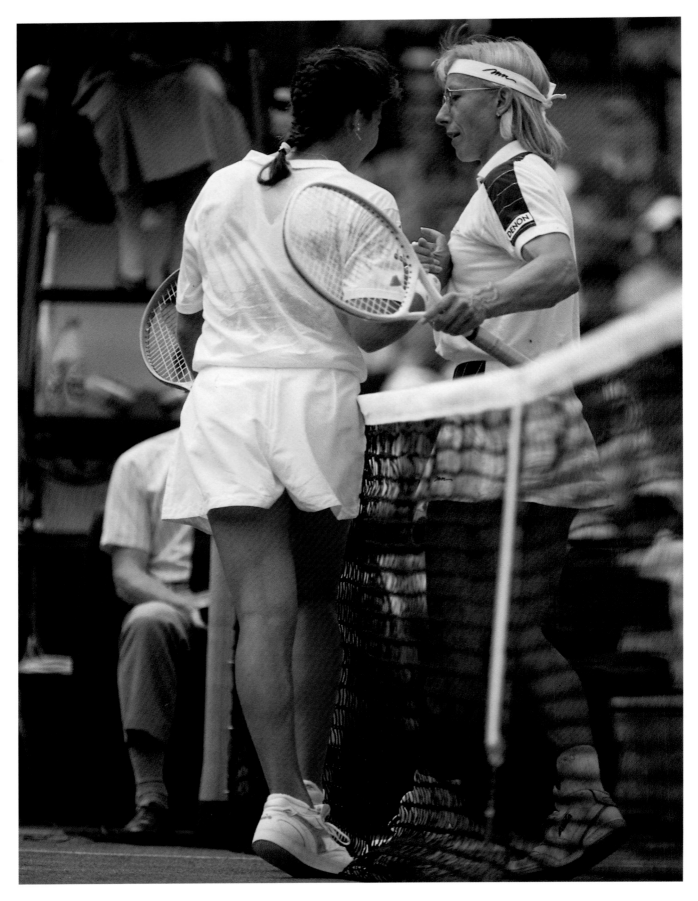

Perhaps if he gave up tennis, André Agassi could become a juggler.

Martina Navratilova, the oldest competitor, masks her disappointment after losing her title in the quarter-finals against the youngest player, Jennifer Capriati.

match point for a third time. Dreadful though the double fault that followed must have been for its perpetrator, it was not, sadly, out of character.

'Now I have to wait another year,' commented Miss Navratilova, still convinced that she can push her record of singles titles into double figures. For Miss Capriati, who had never before beaten an opponent among the world's top five, there was the reward of a semi-final against Gabriela Sabatini, who had also produced her best form of the fortnight as she wound up a 6–2, 6–1 defeat of Laura Gildemeister.

Miss Capriati concluded her shock win about 15 minutes before The Princess of Wales was scheduled to arrive in the Royal Box. 'They told me she would be there at about 1.50 pm and I said, "Well I hope I won't be able to see her. Hopefully the match will be over." ' As Alan Fraser put it in *The Independent*, 'The tennis princess departed and a real one arrived.'

Whatever regrets Miss Navratilova felt about her defeat and her performance, they did not show as she maintained her quest for the four overall titles she needs to beat Billie Jean King's combined singles and doubles list of 20. Within two and a half hours she was back on Centre Court with Pam

Jacco Eltingh won many admirers once he recovered from his slow start against André Agassi.

Colette Hall from Dorset went out in the second round of the girls' singles to Holland's Kristie Boogert.

Ilie Nastase and Roger Taylor (foreground) kept the crowd well entertained despite their 35 and Over Men's Invitation Doubles defeat by former main doubles champions, Bob Hewitt and Frew McMillan.

Yuka Tanaka from Japan beat Sarah Bentley in the first round of the girls' singles. Kristie Boogert (far right), one of the many fine prospects in Dutch tennis, on her way to beating Colette Hall.

Shriver, her partner in five of six previous women's doubles successes, and reaching the quarter-finals with a 6–7, 6–2, 6–2 defeat of the Australians Jo-Anne Faull and Rachael McQuillan.

Boris Becker, after his wasted day 24 hours earlier, when the weather denied him the chance to play, went perilously close to talking himself out of his fourth-round match with the tenacious and impressively quick Swede, Christian Bergstrom, ranked a modest 58 in the world.

For the second consecutive round Becker allowed his mind to wander and his thoughts to fester, before progressing 6–4, 6–7, 6–1, 7–6. As Bergstrom rallied from an early break down to lead 5–3 in the second set, Becker went into what has become an all too familiar routine of haranguing himself – and his racket – as he stalks round the back of the court in abject frustration. The dreadful smash with which he lost a 7–4 tie-break, after he had broken back in the ninth game, did little to improve his demeanour.

Even after romping away with the third set in 24 minutes, with plenty of hefty serves, including two aces in the first game, Becker's mood contin-

ued to be as erratic as his form. He was fortunate that Bergstrom never quite played as if he believed he could win, especially when he served for the fourth set at 5–4 and double-faulted on the second point. Becker went on to break back with a heavy top-spin forehand, which just dropped in at the baseline, forcing his opponent into a cramped and rushed backhand that landed in the net.

Victory took Becker into a quarter-final against Guy Forget, the left-handed Frenchman, who had needed only five minutes to complete a 6–7, 7–5, 6–2, 6–4 win over Tim Mayotte. Meanwhile Thierry Champion, six points from victory overnight, had to play another 17 points to wind up his 6–7, 6–2, 6–1, 3–6, 6–3 defeat of Derrick Rostagno, thus providing France with two quarter-finalists for the first time since 1946, when Yvon Petra, still in long trousers in those days, went on to win the title.

Champion, most unexpected of the quarter-finalists, offered an intriguing explanation for his success. 'I was lucky it rained,' he said. 'I didn't have time to practise serve and volley on grass when I arrived, so I just played my normal game. I guess that's why I'm winning matches.'

Never a dull moment when Henri Leconte is on court. Steffi Graf, his mixed doubles partner, enjoys the fun.

Boris Becker (right) in action against Christian Bergstrom.

Back on Centre Court, André Agassi, who described playing in front of Princess Diana as 'neat – I don't have much experience with royalty watching me play', took the first 12 points before the initially overawed Jacco Eltingh from Holland knew what was happening. In fairness, Eltingh had also played more games than anyone else (162) in the most successful event of his budding career, and the way he recovered from losing the first set in 27 minutes to take the second, with two service breaks, earned him many admirers.

By the end of Agassi's 6–3, 3–6, 6–3, 6–4 win, Eltingh's game tally had reached 199 – 90 more than Edberg, the defending champion, had played at that stage. For two other Dutch players, however, that must have seemed like chicken feed. Michiel Schapers and Brenda Schultz went on court for their first-round mixed doubles match against another Dutchman, Tom Nijssen, and Hungary's Andrea Temesvari at 11.59 am; they did not finish until 4.13 pm, with the score at 6–3, 5–7, 29–27. It was the longest mixed doubles set and match, in terms of games (77), at Wimbledon or any recognized mixed doubles tournament around the world.

Not only that, but Schapers and Miss Schultz then returned to play another 30 games in their second-round match against Rick Leach and Zina Garrison, which was halted by bad light with the score at 3–6, 6–3, 6–6. Yet their total of 107 games in a single day was *not* a Wimbledon record. That dubious honour still rests with Louise Brough. On finals day in 1949, when she became women's singles and women's doubles champion and finished runner-up in the mixed doubles, she played 117 games.

D A Y

10

Thursday 4 July

It was inevitable that some Americans were going to be disappointed on the Fourth of July, and so it proved, both in the semi-finals of the ladies' singles – where neither the precociously gifted Jennifer Capriati nor the resolute Mary Joe Fernandez could continue their earlier successes – and in the delayed quarter-finals of the men's singles, where two of their three players bade farewell.

The one exception was David Wheaton, the leaning tower of Lake Minnetonka, who followed up his defeat of Ivan Lendl by bringing the curtain down on André Agassi's great new love affair with Wimbledon, in one of the most extraordinary contests of the fortnight.

The unashamed sceptics, who had become converts to the all-white showman, gave Agassi yet another standing ovation after his 6–2, 0–6, 3–6, 7–6, 6–2 defeat. During the match he had overcome a dreadful start, and a thigh injury, to reach the point of triumph, before his game and his confidence collapsed when he served for victory at 6–5 in the fourth set.

Agassi, it transpired, had 'felt something tear' when he came down from a serve in the first game. He was twice treated by the LTA's physiotherapist, John Matthews, who applied a heavy strapping to the right thigh, during a first set that Wheaton took in 25 minutes.

'I was thinking about giving up from the third game,' said Agassi. 'Had it been any other occa-

sion I probably would have done so, but for all they have given me' – with reference to the adoring crowd – 'the thought of giving them something back was important.'

Far from becoming demoralized, Agassi launched into high-octane spells of brilliant returns, which not only spectacularly turned things round but left Wheaton bemused, until at 0–40 he was three points away from being broken to go 2–5 down in the fourth set. Suddenly Wheaton produced five great first services, including two aces, to escape. For Agassi, even though he served for the match four games later, that was the turning point.

Agassi, beaten in the finals of the last three Grand Slam tournaments in which he had played during the previous 13 months, came within two points of victory at 30–15 in the 12th game, but then disastrously delivered only his second double fault. An even more careless forehand followed, and from then on the energy drained from him like a burst main. His first credible Wimbledon visit had ended in sadness and some pain, but also with many happy memories and a promise that he would be back. 'I think England and myself were both a little unsure what to expect, but it turned out quite well,' he said.

Wheaton, ranked 20th in the world but probably worthy of one of the top six places on grass, took the fourth-set tie-break (which was full of Agassi backhand errors) 7–3, and yet another backhand blunder allowed him to forge ahead from the first game of the final set. Of those five enormous serves he had produced just when they were most needed, he later said, 'I think it takes Wimbledon for that to happen.'

The first American to reach the semi-finals unseeded since Tim Mayotte in 1982, Wheaton had certainly had a narrow escape. But so too had his next opponent, Boris Becker, who continued to make life extraordinarily difficult both for himself and his supporters, by toiling for 3 hours 47 minutes under the hot Court 1 sun to beat Guy Forget 6–7, 7–6, 6–2, 7–6.

The seventh-seeded Frenchman, though happy to have gone further than ever before in the tournament, was inwardly furious with himself

The strain showed on André Agassi's face as his new-found romance with Wimbledon came to an end after an early injury against David Wheaton.

Boris Becker faced so many service winners from Guy Forget, before beating the Frenchman, that he briefly decided to take cover.

It was still nice and straightforward for Stefan Edberg, who beat Thierry Champion and reached the semi-finals without the loss of a set.

Jim Courier's Wimbledon flourish was brought to an end in the quarter-finals as Michael Stich reversed their result at the French Open.

Jennifer Capriati continued to enjoy herself on the Centre Court even though she ran out of energy against Gabriela Sabatini.

Gabriela Sabatini mops her brow after one of several fine, exhausting rallies against Jennifer Capriati.

for not having at least stretched Becker into a fifth set – and a fifth hour. 'If I had won two points at crucial stages, I would have taken the match in four sets instead of losing it in four,' he observed despondently. 'I was more consistent than him in the whole match, but he played two or three big points better than me – and that's what counts.'

Forget served 24 aces to Becker's 16 and sustained his attacking ferocity in a manner that even his opponent admired. 'That's something I've not seen in a long time,' said Becker. 'Someone who can serve like that for so long. Thank God it wasn't longer.'

There were few rallies. Not that many people expected there to be. And there was the hint of a bitter taste when, at 3–5 in the fourth set, Becker took a three-minute time-out for treatment on a knee he had cut in a fall a set earlier. Forget, clearly irritated by the delay, just before he would try and serve for the match, was broken after netting two straightforward volleys. He flung down his racket and was warned for racket abuse.

Forget had three more chances at 6–3 in the tie-

Virginia Wade, the 1977 champion – successfully partnering Wendy Turnbull in the 35 and Over Ladies' Invitation Doubles – can still show others the way.

break and yet another at 7–6, so suddenly, from being in the driving seat, he found himself, at 6–7, match point down. Like Miss Navratilova the day before, Forget then double-faulted. Not only that, but the ball remained lodged in the top of the net, as a lingering, painful reminder.

While Becker continued to struggle, Edberg once more looked invincible, although one needed to remember that Thierry Champion's baseline game, which might have been too consistent for earlier rivals, was not likely to prove more than a token challenge to the defending champion. Edberg won 6–3, 6–2, 7–5 in 1 hour 41 minutes, leaving an admiring Champion to concur, after failing to come up with a more suitable English term, that 'Yes, Edberg is a machine.'

The fourth quarter-final, to provide Edberg with his next opponent, was a re-run of the French Open semi-final. Then, in accordance with expectations on a clay court, Jim Courier beat Michael Stich. This time Stich, riding an enormous crest of a serving wave, gained revenge, as was also expected, 6–3, 7–6, 6–2, to give Germany two semifinalists in the men's singles for the first time ever.

Stich added another 16 aces to the 61 he had already hit in four previous matches. 'His serving was just monstrous,' said Courier. 'And his returns were pretty effective as well.'

When asked if he could go on to win the tournament, Stich smiled and replied, 'Why not?'

Defeats for Mary Joe Fernandez and Jennifer Capriati, the new standard-bearers for women's tennis in the United States, meant that, for the first time since Virginia Wade beat Betty Stove in the centenary year of The Championships in 1977, there would be no American in the final.

Instead, it would be Steffi Graf versus Gabriela Sabatini, the top two seeds (following the withdrawal of Monica Seles) – and more than appropriate inasmuch as their rivalry, more than any other, has succeeded the long-running Navratilova-Evert saga.

Barely 24 hours after she had knocked out Miss Navratilova, Miss Capriati did not have quite enough mental or physical energy left to produce another supreme effort. Whereas against the 1990 champion many of the points were short, Miss Capriati found that Miss Sabatini had the patience to rally, the occasional wit to slip in drop shots or lobs, and, above all, the ability to pass an opponent who was neither as consistent nor as aggressive as the day before.

Miss Sabatini won 6–4, 6–4, but as she moved close to victory, at 4–1 in the second set, she became ominously nervous, especially on a serve that had already been broken three times in her first eight service games. The danger signals for the final were there for those shrewd enough to see them. It looked all over when Miss Capriati, 3–5 down, trailed 0–40, but that became the finest game of the match, for she saved the three match points with two forehand winners – one crosscourt, the other down the line – and then a bold backhand volley, on the way to holding serve. She also took the first two points of the next game, before her forehand broke down again and a relieved Miss Sabatini claimed her place in the Wimbledon final for the first time.

Miss Graf took 1 hour 20 minutes to beat Miss Fernandez 6–2, 6–4, but she knew she had not really been impressive. 'When it was important, I played better,' she said. 'But I wasn't aggressive enough and I also made more mistakes than usual. I was missing a little bit of something.'

She was perhaps fortunate that Miss Fernandez, especially in a first set that was closer than 6–2 would suggest (including a third game of nine minutes and nine deuces) was not quite bold enough to take the initiative more often. Excluding service returns, Miss Graf made 17 unforced errors on her forehand, and yet every time one felt that they might be her undoing, the forehand became her ace in the pack again.

Those great Dutch record-breakers, Michiel Schapers and Brenda Schultz, kept winning. They not only completed their unfinished final set against Rick Leach and Zina Garrison 13–11, but then beat Sven Salumaa and Karin Kschwendt 3–6, 6–2, 6–1, playing a mere 37 games compared with 107 the day before. It must have seemed like a day off.

British hopes that Jeremy Bates and Jo Durie might match their success in Australia, where they won the mixed doubles title in January, by repeating their 1987 Wimbledon triumph, ended when they were beaten 7–5, 6–4 in the third round by the top seeds, Jim Pugh and Natalia Zvereva.

The hopes of former mixed doubles champions, Jo Durie and Jeremy Bates, foundered against eventual runners-up Jim Pugh and Natalia Zvereva.

(Overleaf) A spectacular view of Court 1 as Boris Becker serves against Christian Bergstrom.

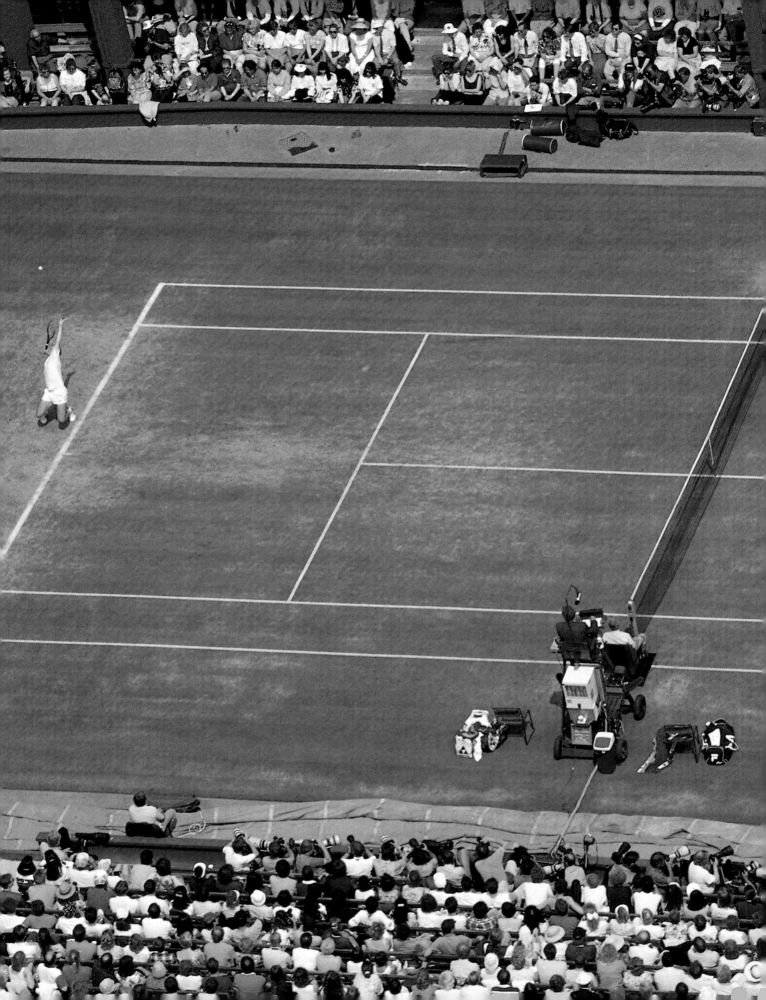

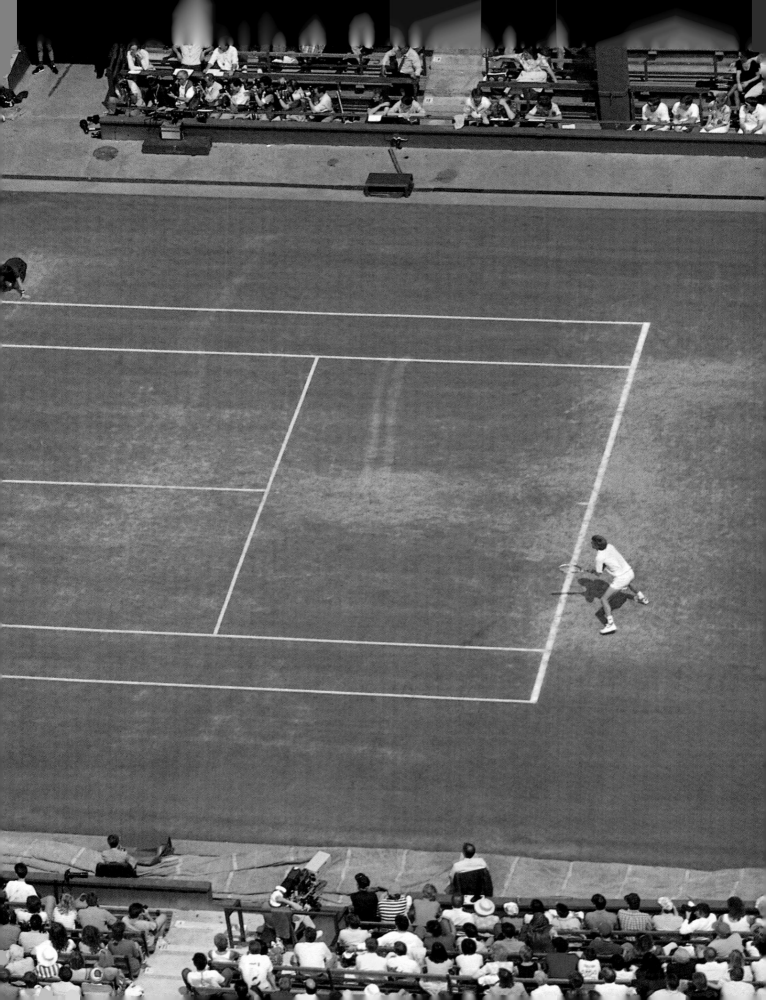

D A Y

11

Friday 5 July

It was on the eve of the men's singles semi-finals that the news came through of the sudden death, after a fall at his home in Newport, Rhode Island, of Jimmy Van Alen, the man who introduced the tie-break, which Wimbledon adopted (although, thankfully, not for final sets) in 1979.

There was more than a touch of irony, therefore, that in the first of the semi-finals Stefan Edberg, the 1990 champion and an acknowledged master of the serve and volley, should become the first player to lose at such a late stage in The Championships without once dropping his serve – after losing three tie-break sets.

Even so, it was not the tie-break system so much as some surprising errors by Edberg that led to the London-based Swedish player's reign as champion coming to a shuddering halt, just when he appeared to be moving imperiously to his fourth consecutive final against Boris Becker.

Later in the day Becker did his bit, beating David Wheaton 6–4, 7–6, 7–5 to reach his sixth final in seven years, but Edberg went down 4–6, 7–6, 7–6, 7–6 to Michael Stich, to produce the first all-German men's final in any Grand Slam tournament.

'It is the most beautiful thing that could have happened,' said Stich. 'Losing or winning, it will be great for us to have two Germans in the final,' continued the player who showed such admirable concentration and consistency to earn the opportunity to add the greatest title to the only other one

Stefan Edberg, under serious pressure for the first time – and eventually beaten by Michael Stich even though the German never once managed to break his service.

David Wheaton cannot believe his bad luck as one of ten break points eludes him in his semi-final against Boris Becker.

These Service personnel had more than a glimpse of David Wheaton against Boris Becker.

'Of course I think I can win . . . otherwise I should be on my way to the next tournament,' Michael Stich kept saying – and proving.

he had collected so far – at Memphis in February a year earlier.

Stich admitted that 'Sometimes it's just luck to win three tie-breaks in a row.' He had never done so before. For Edberg, it was the first time he had lost in such a manner. 'And I hope it never happens again,' he added ruefully.

Reflecting on what was clearly a grim disappointment, after he had not only never lost his serve but only had three break points against him, Edberg agreed that he did not play well enough on the most important points. He singled out the poor service return he struck at 5–5 in the third-set tie-break, in which he had led 4–2. That error left him facing a set point, which he lost because he took his eye off a challenging, but by no means unbeatable, Stich lob, and made no more than a thin-edge connection off the top of the racket, as he went for the smash.

Even so, the seeds of uncertainty had been present one tie-break earlier in a match in which, for

All smiles between Zina Garrison (left) and Mary Joe Fernandez, despite their defeat by Gigi Fernandez and Jana Novotna in the semi-finals of the women's doubles.

'Don't worry, Martina, I've got you covered,' Pam Shriver seems to be telling her partner – but the former champions were beaten by Larissa Savchenko and Natalia Zvereva in the semi-finals.

114

No easy escape for Martina Navratilova after the doubles defeat that left her without a Wimbledon finals appearance for the first time in ten years.

so much of the time, it was stalemate between two players who both serve and return better than most. A spectacularly dreadful double fault in the second-set tie-break was reminiscent of the two from which Edberg was fortunate that Becker had allowed him to escape, in the last set of the 1990 final.

Although Edberg immediately responded with a big service down the middle to deny Stich the set point he had been offered, the German still had another to play, and this time Edberg's service return was long. Edberg's authority, which had looked so thorough before the second-set tie-break, especially as until then he had dropped only eight points on his own eleven service games, was never the same again.

While the steadily more perplexed champion began to have problems with his toss and the subsequent timing of his serves, Stich's great strength was the pace and variety of his second serves, plus a wonderfully cool nerve under pressure.

The third set, like the second, went with serve, with not even a break point until 5–5, when a clear buzz went round Centre Court as Edberg's serve was seriously threatened for the only time. He

escaped magnificently from 0–40, with the help of three strident serves, and when he later went down on one knee in joy after a glorious backhand pass down the line, which put him 4–2 ahead in the tie-break, he must once more have felt that the match would be his.

It was not to be. In the tie-break at the end of the fourth set the German won the first point with a backhand volley at full stretch – which caught the sideline – and the third point with a net cord. Another Stich ace hastened the end.

'I feel I lost it. I thought I gave it away,' said Edberg. 'There wasn't much difference between us; there were just three or four points which cost me the match, but I blew the chances I had.' The defeat also cost him his number one world ranking, which went back to Becker.

Becker, despite a strapped right thigh and a plaster below his right knee, saved a total of ten break points, twice from 0–40, most crucially at 4–4 in the third set, giving at least some substance to Wheaton's greatly exaggerated claim to have 'outplayed' the German. The key, in fact, was that under pressure Becker served quite brilliantly and underlined his class with the magnificent forehand service return he struck on match point. It was almost as if, despite his complaints about the scheduling, he knew he clearly had plenty in reserve. Impressions, though, as everyone in

John Lloyd kept British interest alive right through to the final of the 35 and Over Men's Invitation Singles.

tennis knows, can be dangerously misleading.

Meanwhile Martina Navratilova suffered another setback to her burning ambition to break more Wimbledon records, when she and Pam Shriver started the day with a 6–3, 7–6 doubles victory over Arantxa Sanchez Vicario and Helena Sukova on Court 1 but then ran out of energy, as well as inspiration, in their semi-final on a packed Court 14, where they were beaten 2–6, 6–2, 6–4 by the Soviet pair, Larissa Savchenko and Natalia Zvereva. They, as the seedings decreed, would be meeting Gigi Fernandez and Jana Novotna in the final.

In the men's doubles the unseeded pair, Javier Frana from Argentina and Leonardo Lavalle (a former Wimbledon junior champion) from Mexico, continued to flourish, this time at the expense of 15th-seeded Wayne Ferreira and Pavel Norval. The former pair won 6–2, 6–4, 7–6 to qualify for the final against the 1989 champions Anders Jarryd and John Fitzgerald.

The number two seeds conceded their first set of the tournament while overcoming the Canadians, Grant Connell (famous for his day with André Agassi) and Glenn Michibata, 6–2, 6–7, 7–6, 6–4. Connell was still involved in the mixed doubles with Kathy Rinaldi, but while they were winning their quarter-final, the great run by Michiel Schapers and Brenda Schultz was being brought to an end by the unseeded South Africans, Christo Van Rensburg and Elna Reinach. No one was surprised, after what had gone before, that the Dutch pair went down after only two tie-breaks.

One of the great treats for Wimbledon crowds in the second week of The Championships is wandering around the outside courts catching another nostalgic look at some of the great names of the past. Some – like John Newcombe and Tony Roche, in losing 6–3, 6–4 to Nikki Pilic and Balazs Taroczy, and the ever-carefree Ilie Nastase, partnering Roger Taylor against the still deadly serious Bob Hewitt and Frew McMillan – also made it on to the show courts. One pair in whom there was special interest were the Czechoslovakians, Pavel Slozil and Tomas Smid, who beat Ken Rosewall and Fred Stolle to reach the semi-finals. They had something else in common: the players they were coaching, Steffi Graf and Boris Becker, were both possibly one match away from regaining their singles titles. Only Slozil, though (coaching Miss Graf), was to have compensation for losing in Sunday's final to Peter McNamara and Paul McNamee.

D A Y

12

Saturday 6 July

Steffi Graf made sure it would be a *wunderbar* final weekend for German tennis at Wimbledon – but only just. At almost precisely 4 pm, on a fine sunny Saturday afternoon, Gabriela Sabatini was serving for the title she had dreamt of winning for a whole year. Less than 20 minutes later she could do no more than join in the generous applause as Miss Graf held up the gleaming trophy for a third time.

In a memorably tense and exciting climax to a match that had actually benefited in such terms from a host of nervously erratic errors, the top seed suddenly and decisively lifted her game for a 6–4, 3–6, 8–6 victory, after twice being allowed back into the contest by her opponent's frail serving.

'This is so special to me. It means so much and I needed it so badly,' said Miss Graf, immediately grasping at the security of knowing that, for the time being at least, her victory would silence those who believed that a career that once looked as if it would know no bounds might have been irreparably damaged by the events surrounding her life in the previous 18 months.

The Princess of Wales and her eldest son, Prince William, whom Miss Graf told later she would be delighted to coach – if his first Wimbledon visit led to him wanting to emulate his mother's enthusiasm for lawn tennis – were among the packed Centre Court crowd watching the German win her 10th Grand Slam tournament title. And this only four weeks after her world seemed to be in ruins, when she collapsed so

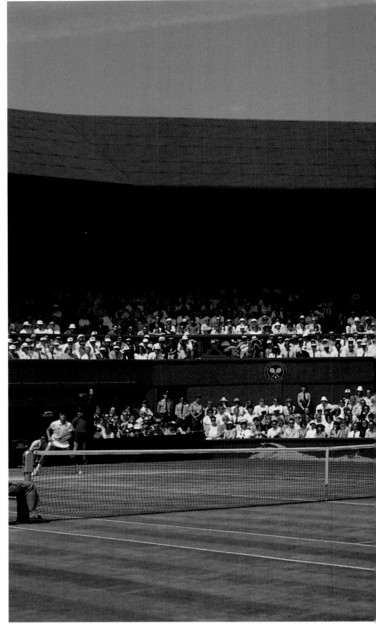

Steffi Graf's match-winning forehand.

So near and yet so far for Gabriela Sabatini (left) in the face of Steffi Graf's serve and awesome forehand, which played a key role as she eventually experienced that glorious moment of triumph again, enabling her to hold the trophy aloft for a third time.

Steffi Graf delights in becoming the champion again.

meekly in the semi-finals of the French Open.

In the end, she was just marginally stronger and bolder than Miss Sabatini in a contest of just over two hours, in which, for a tantalizing spell in that final set, both players did more to help the other than themselves. The last time they had met in a Grand Slam final, at the US Open the previous September, Miss Sabatini had won with precisely the attacking style that her coach, Carlo Kirmayr, had convinced her would also make it possible for her to win Wimbledon.

When she looks back on Wimbledon '91, Miss Sabatini will know that she could have done so. Considering that she had won her last five matches against Miss Graf before this one, Miss Sabatini's early form was neither auspicious nor comforting. There were hardly any attempts to take command at the net in the first set, when Miss Graf, cleverly using the full width of the court with her fore-hands, safely maintained the service break she achieved for 3–2 in the first set, just as her father, Peter, arrived in the players' box.

When Miss Graf, bouncing on her toes and quicker in thought and deed than her opponent, broke again in the opening game of the second set, she literally skipped to her chair in delight. By contrast, Miss Sabatini walked slowly, even dejectedly, round the net.

Yet, just as it looked as if Miss Graf might steamroller on, she ran into a spell of errors. A double fault gave the Argentinian her first break-point, which she held because Miss Graf's next forehand flew wide. At last Miss Sabatini began to allow her tennis to match the weather, and the crowd's approval was obvious as she swept, some-times majestically, to a 5–2 lead, with Miss Graf frequently changing rackets in an attempt to find the formula that would enable her to stem the tide.

Nevertheless, it was only after she had broken back from 0–2 in the third set that Miss Sabatini – at least until it came to serving for the match – really attacked with relish, rather than as a duty. The match certainly should have been hers after the ninth game, when she broke as Miss Graf lifted her head – and the ball – under pressure from her net-rushing opponent and, on the next point, double-faulted. When it was put to the test, how-ever, Miss Sabatini's serve looked so feeble in this class of tennis that it undermined all the effort that had gone before.

Miss Graf broke straight back to 15 and then, after losing her own serve once more in the 11th

game, netting a forehand volley with the court wide open, more timid serves by Miss Sabatini invited more severe return punishment. At 30–30, with the Argentinian two points from the title, there came the finest point of the match, involving a high, leaping backhand volley from Miss Sabatini that initially looked to be a winner, and much resilient running and retrieving on the other side of the net. Miss Graf finally took the point with a backhand winner, and said later that it was probably also the biggest point of the match.

Another weak serve gave Miss Graf the chance to break back again and, having held to 30, she then took Miss Sabatini's serve once more, encouraged by a net cord on the first point of the final game, which she went on to win. The Graf family was all smiles again. The Sabatini camp did not look too dismayed. They just pledged more work on that serve.

Miss Graf, who flew home for the night to watch her brother in a car race the next day, before returning to London for The Champions' Dinner, perhaps provided the perfect analysis of the final when she said, 'It wasn't the highest standard of tennis. But now, I think, everything will change for me.'

Certainly the opportunity had been created.

Meanwhile the always popular John Fitzgerald, who was to become the only player this year to finish with more than one of the five principal titles, completed the first part of his splendid double (incidentally, worth £70,000 to him) by partnering Anders Jarryd to success in the final of the men's doubles.

It was the second men's doubles triumph at Wimbledon for this experienced Australian-Swedish combination in three years and followed their victory at the French Open four weeks earlier. They beat the unseeded Latin Americans, Javier Frana and Leonardo Lavalle, 6–3, 6–4, 6–7, 6–1 in nearly two and a half hours, although it should have been settled much sooner.

The first set, in which Frana's service was broken, was over in a quick-fire 25 minutes and the second, when again the greater sharpness of Fitzgerald and Jarryd at the net proved decisive, did not take much longer. But the second seeds lost four break points against Lavalle in the ninth game of the third set, and also a match point in the tie-break, which their unseeded and increasingly optimistic challengers took 9–7.

When Jarryd was broken in the first game of

Jim Thorn casts a farewell eye round Centre Court.

Unorthodox, but none the less effective. That summed up this point for John Fitzgerald and Anders Jarryd (left) as they regained the men's doubles trophy.

(Overleaf) Steffi Graf and men's doubles winners, Anders Jarryd and John Fitzgerald, with their trophies.

the fourth set an even longer struggle looked in prospect, but then he and the exuberant Fitzgerald stepped up the tempo in exhilarating style to take six consecutive games – for the title. Not that Fitzgerald's day was over. He and Liz Smylie were soon back on court, clearing the mixed doubles backlog with a rapid 6–4, 6–2 quarter-final win in the twilight over fellow Australians, Jason Stoltenberg and Rennae Stubbs.

Hopes of playing at least the semi-final in the top half of the mixed doubles draw that day were thwarted because Natalia Zvereva, who would be partnering Jim Pugh against Grant Connell and Kathy Rinaldi, was needed for what became an exciting women's doubles final, which kept a still-sizeable Centre Court crowd entertained and enthralled until 9.18 pm.

Miss Zvereva and Larissa Savchenko, runners-up in 1980 and 1989, looked doomed to further disappointment when they lost their way badly in the second set and the top seeds, Jana Novotna and Gigi Fernandez, moved into a 4–2 lead in the third set. But then Miss Novotna's game suddenly crumbled and the Soviet pair, ecstatic at the end of their 6–4, 3–6, 6–4 triumph, took four consecutive games, ending with a Novotna double fault.

Another, earlier highlight of the day had been on Court 1, where Britain's John Lloyd, 37, fought his way into the final of the 35 and Over Men's Invitation Singles by beating Tom Gullikson, the holder, 7–6, 3–6, 7–5. The loud cheers wafting over the adjoining Centre Court during the women's singles final reflected the excitement and outcome of that match.

D A Y

13

Sunday 7 July

Michael Stich slumped slowly to his knees, hardly knowing whether to laugh or cry with joy, after hitting the winning forehand service return that made him probably the most unexpected Wimbledon champion there has been among the 12 proud holders of the trophy since professionals were first allowed to compete in 1968.

Stich, 22, still 'Michael who?' to the many who had not noticed him sweep up the world rankings from 42nd to seventh, on his way to Wimbledon, simply could not believe it. Nor, one imagines, could Boris Becker, the three-times former champion and overwhelming favourite on the day, who had just been beaten in straight sets for the first time in 46 Wimbledon matches over eight always memorable years.

A few days before The Championships, the odds against Stich – a complete novice at this sort of occasion, despite his semi-final at Roland Garros – had been quoted as high as 60–1 by some bookmakers. That compared with odds of 12–1 against Becker in 1985 when he became the first unseeded, as well as the youngest, champion, because he had clearly provided some advance warning of his major challenge by winning at Queen's Club. Stich stole through, at least to the last eight, while almost no one was looking properly.

'When Boris won for the first time, that was the first time I paid attention to Wimbledon, although I didn't know him then,' said the slim but immensely powerful young man, as he proudly displayed the most coveted tennis trophy in the world, after a richly deserved 6–4, 7–6, 6–4 triumph.

As expected, the style of the match was hardly memorable. It was mainly a case of prolonged attrition between two players whose first priority seemed to be to blast one another off court, if not with their first serves, then with their returns. Or, as the ever-wise last British champion, Fred Perry, observed, 'Too much biff and bang with too few rallies for spectators to get their teeth into.'

The pre-match statistics provided a foretaste of what to expect. Stich had delivered his fastest Centre Court serve of the tournament against Edberg (125 miles per hour), while Becker's best had been only three miles an hour slower. Becker had struck 89 aces compared with Stich's 82, but had also double-faulted more (46–34) and had not been so productive off second serves as had his new rival for the headlines in German tennis.

Clearly it was going to boil down to the greatest mental, as well as physical, strength and durability. Stich, with nothing to lose, took the honours on all counts. He hit another 15 aces to take his official, though disputed, total (because some had recorded even more) to 97, two fewer over the fortnight than Becker; and on returns, especially off his backhand, which was brilliant, Stich outnumbered his Davis Cup team-mate overwhelmingly.

Even as recently as two months beforehand, in Hamburg, Stich, a late developer who had stayed at school until he was 18, was questioning his own resolve. Yet it was also the German Open, where beating Edberg for the first time was something of a breakthrough, that his coach, Mark Lewis (brother of the 1983 Wimbledon runner-up, Chris), regards as the moment when Stich really began to believe in himself.

Certainly his coolness on the big points was a constant feature of the success he claimed by becoming only the third German – after the late Michael Westphal and Carl-Uwe Steeb – to have beaten Becker. And Becker himself has done more than anyone to inspire other German players to have broader horizons than was often the case in the 1970s and early 1980s.

Michael Stich on his way to the greatest moment of his tennis life .

128

Boris Becker stumbled once too often.

Stich's instant response after reading the newspapers on the morning of the final and discovering that, almost without exception, they expected Becker to win, was to break his opponent's serve in the opening game with the first of many fierce backhand service returns. Although Becker broke back to 3–3 with one of the best games he played, he promptly double-faulted twice, before being broken again by that ferocious Stich backhand.

'In the final, tactics alone are not that important. It's who has the strongest mind. He had. Mine was far away,' said Becker after his third defeat in the final in four years. It was while Stich was firmly holding on to his second chance to take the first set that Becker could no longer mask the corrosive thoughts of self-doubt, which were already in his troubled mind.

They manifested themselves again in noisily irritating and sometimes ill-tempered outbursts, as he prowled round the court like a caged tiger. The barriers were all of his own making, however – and counter-productive. At one time he screamed in German, 'I don't want to be here. I want to get off.'

Stich did not mind. 'I could see how angry and frustrated he was getting. He expected too much of himself and that built up my confidence. "Okay," I said to myself, "let's beat him."'

Having wasted that key recovery chance in the first set, Becker repeated the felony in the second, when he broke for 3–1, but Stich hit two more

The moment of ecstasy.

The awful moment of truth for Boris Becker (left). Michael Stich's joy is clear for all to see as he accepts congratulations from his opponent after the first all-German men's singles final.

(Overleaf) Michael Stich with the winner's trophy as (inset) Boris Becker acknowledges the sympathy of the crowd.

explosive backhand winners to break back again one game later. And the tie-break that decided this set perfectly illustrated the sturdy resilience of one man and the brittle carelessness of the other.

On the first point Becker missed the easiest of shoulder-high volleys, with the court wide open. Stich, though pegged back to 1–1, broke again for 3–1 with another of those remorseless backhands and went on to reach set points with a great second serve, before taking the first of them with his 11th ace.

A year earlier, Becker nearly won from two sets down against Edberg. On this occasion it was only a matter of time before he would lose. He served well enough to save three break points in the fourth game and then to save another in the eighth, but two games later there was no escape.

Becker explained that he had been mentally tired, and he seemed to want to place at least some of the blame on the match scheduling, which, he complained, 'always seemed to make me last on the list to play'. In truth, however, in a year when the weather made it impossible to keep to the desired daily programme, Becker suffered more from his shortage of competitive match play, for various reasons, in the three months before The Championships.

Just as Stich had prepared immaculately for each match that had edged him closer and closer to a title which, in his wildest dreams, he could not really have expected to win at this stage of his career – and he might not have done so, but for that fourth-round net cord against Alexander Volkov – so he had taken one other important precaution. On the Friday after beating Stefan Edberg he had hired a dinner jacket ... just in case it was needed.

As he said, 'If you reach a final and don't feel confident you can win it, you should pack up and move to the next tournament.' The dinner jacket was needed and, during The Champions' Dinner, when Stich posed alongside a radiant Steffi Graf in double-German celebration, he was also presented by The All England Club Chairman, John Curry, with the Club tie, which confirmed his membership of the most famous tennis club in the world.

'It's not exactly the easiest way to join, but it's the best way,' Miss Graf told him. Michael clearly needed no convincing about that.

Meanwhile, between the men's singles final and the dinner, there had still been much to settle,

Tim Gullikson kept the 35 and Over Men's Invitation Singles title in the family by winning the event that his brother won a year earlier.

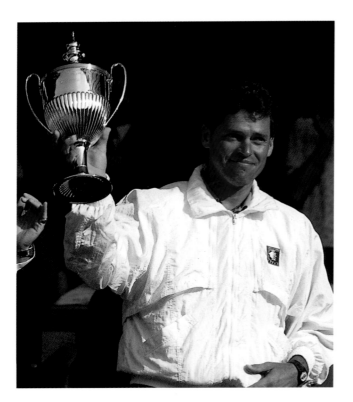

including the final of the mixed doubles, to which both teams, John Fitzgerald and Liz Smylie versus Jim Pugh and Natalia Zvereva, had won their way through semi-finals earlier in the day. In the final there was no hint of a service break until both women dropped their serves to produce a tie-break, which the Australians won 7–4.

By contrast, there were four service breaks in the first five games of the second set, but then Fitzgerald held for 4–2 and he and Mrs Smylie, runners-up in 1985 and 1990, went on to win 7–5, 6–2.

Elsewhere there was an opportunity to muse on the future and to wallow in memories from the past. Thomas Enqvist, 17, but already 6 ft 2 in, suggested that the Swedish conveyor belt is still producing smoothly, when he added to his success in the juniors' title at the Australian Open and to being runner-up for a second successive year at the French, by winning the junior boys' title. Enqvist – in the Anders Jarryd style of volatile, rather than unemotional, Swedes – came through his toughest challenge in the quarter-finals against the American Vincent Spadea. And it was against another American, the unseeded Michael Joyce, who had beaten top seed Karim Alami from Morocco in the second round, that Enqvist served powerfully and hit huge forehands to take the trophy, 6–4, 6–3. Now all he has to aim to do is

Canada's Greg Rusedski (left) and Morocco's Karim Alami hold aloft the boys' doubles trophy.

John Fitzgerald and Liz Smylie proudly display the mixed doubles trophy.

emulate the performances of his illustrious countrymen, Bjorn Borg (1972) and Stefan Edberg (1983), by one day winning the main event as well.

Germany's 1991 Wimbledon celebrations did not end with Michael Stich and Steffi Graf. Also toasted at The Champions' Dinner was Barbara Rittner, 18, already 73rd in the women's world rankings, who had plenty of time, after losing in the first round of the singles to Arantxa Sanchez Vicario, to concentrate on winning the junior girls' title. It was no easy task. She dropped a set in three of her matches, including the final, when she outlasted Elena Makarova of the USSR, 6–7, 6–2, 6–3.

Andrei Medvedev, Russian winner of the boys' singles in Paris, had gone out in the third round of the juniors' singles but had some compensation when, in an interesting political partnership with South Africa's John-Laffnie De Jager, he reached the final of the boys' doubles, before losing to Alami and Canada's Greg Rusedski, 1–6, 7–6, 6–4. Catherine Barclay from Australia and Limor Zaltz of Israel, the fourth seeds, won the girls' doubles title by beating the second seeds, Joanne Limmer and Angie Woolcock, both from Australia, 6–4, 6–4, in the final.

Meanwhile, to the relaxed pleasure of those who prefer tennis at a less frantic pace and with not quite so much power, Tim Gullikson and John

Catherine Barclay (left) from Australia and Israel's Limor Zaltz with the girls' doubles trophy.

Thomas Enqvist, junior boys' winner from Sweden, following in the footsteps of Bjorn Borg and Stefan Edberg.

Lloyd provided the ideal liqueur with three sets of lively and good-natured tennis in the final of the 35 and Over Men's Invitation Singles, before Tim at last won the prize that has so often eluded him (twice having lost to his brother Tom in the finals), 7–6, 3–6, 6–2. The 35 and Over Ladies' Invitation Doubles was won again by Wendy Turnbull and Virginia Wade who, in a repeat of the 1990 final, beat the Americans Rosie Casals and Sharon Walsh-Pete, 6–3, 6–4, taking one game more than they needed the previous year.

So ended a Wimbledon, which, at one time, it seemed might never end but which, as always at the finish, you were sorry had come to an end. The crowds had totalled 378,411, an increase of 30,432 on the previous year, thanks principally to the middle Sunday. No one had really wanted that to end either.

CHAMPIONSHIP
RECORDS 1991

LIST OF COMPETITORS

Bold figures denote position in Singles Draw

LADIES'

— Adams, Miss K. M. (U.S.A.)
2 Appelmans, Miss S. (Belgium)
— Bakkum, Miss C. (Netherlands)
— Baranski, Mrs. R. (U.S.A.)
— Barnard, Miss L. (South Africa)
39 Bartos, Miss C. (Switzerland)
— Bassett-Seguso, Mrs. C. K. (Canada)
8 Basuki, Miss Y. (Indonesia)
— Benjamin, Miss C. (U.S.A.)
89 Bentley, Miss S. L. (Great Britain)
21 Bollegraf, Miss M. M. (Netherlands)
13 Bonsignori, Miss F. (Italy)
30 Borneo, Miss B. A. (Great Britain)
70 Brioukhovets, Miss E. (U.S.S.R.)
— Budarova, Miss I. (Czechoslovakia)
— Burgin, Miss E. M. (U.S.A.)
75 Callens, Miss E. (Belgium)
80 Capriati, Miss J. (U.S.A.)
46 Caverzasio, Miss C. (Switzerland)
81 Cecchini, Miss A. M. (Italy)
50 Cioffi, Miss H. (U.S.A.)
36 Coetzer, Miss A. J. (South Africa)
— Collins, Miss S. L. (U.S.A.)
— Coorengel, Miss G. E. (Netherlands)
— Cordwell, Miss B. J. (New Zealand)
122 Cunningham, Miss C. E. (U.S.A.)
88 Dahlman, Miss C. (Sweden)
120 Date, Miss K. (Japan)
59 De Lone, Miss E. (U.S.A.)
106 De Swardt, Miss M. (South Africa)
93 Dechaume, Miss A. (France)
85 Demongeot, Miss I. (France)
23 Durie, Miss J. M. (Great Britain)
45 Faber, Miss D. L. (U.S.A.)
101 Fairbank-Nideffer, Mrs. R. D. (U.S.A.)
41 Faull, Miss J.-A. (Australia)
118 Fendick, Miss P. A. (U.S.A.)
47 Fernandez, Miss G. (Puerto Rico)
64 Fernandez, Miss M. J. (U.S.A.)
119 Ferrando, Miss L. (Italy)
— Field, Miss L. (Australia)
16 Frazier, Miss A. (U.S.A.)
60 Fulco, Miss B. (Argentina)
32 Garrison, Miss Z. L. (U.S.A.)

91 Garrone, Miss L. (Italy)
108 Gildemeister, Mrs. L. (Peru)
42 Godridge, Miss K. (Australia)
62 Golarsa, Miss L. (Italy)
31 Gomer, Miss S. L. (Great Britain)
1 Graf, Miss S. (Germany)
11 Graham, Miss D. A. (U.S.A.)
— Gregory, Miss L. J. (South Africa)
53 Griffiths, Miss B. (Great Britain)
100 Grossman, Miss A. (U.S.A.)
94 Grunfeld, Miss A. L. (Great Britain)
— Guse, Miss K.-A (Australia)
87 Habsudova, Miss K. (Czechoslovakia)
9 Halard, Miss J. (France)
99 Hand, Miss K. D. (Great Britain)
4 Harper, Mrs. T. A. (U.S.A.)
109 Harvey-Wild, Miss L. M. (U.S.A.)
121 Helgeson, Miss G. (U.S.A.)
7 Henricksson, Miss A. B. (U.S.A.)
6 Herreman, Miss N. (France)
117 Hetherington, Miss J. M. (Canada)
28 Hiraki, Miss R. (Japan)
17 Huber, Miss A. (Germany)
22 Humphreys-Davies, Miss V. S. (Great Britain)
102 Hy, Miss P. (Canada)
— Iida, Miss E. (Japan)
55 Jagerman, Miss N. A. M. (Netherlands)
— Jaggard, Miss M. (Australia)
— Jankovska, Miss N. (Czechoslovakia)
127 Javer, Miss M. (Great Britain)
— Jones, Miss D. J. (Australia)
— Jordan, Miss K. (U.S.A.)
63 Kamstra, Miss P. (Netherlands)
24 Kelesi, Miss H. (Canada)
61 Keller, Miss A. A. (U.S.A.)
90 Kidowaki, Miss M. (Japan)
115 Kijimuta, Miss A. (Japan)
54 Kohde-Kilsch, Miss C. (Germany)
110 Kreiss, Mrs. T. J. (U.S.A.)
15 Kschwendt, Miss K. (Luxembourg)
— Lake, Miss V. (Great Britain)
37 Langrova, Miss P. (Czechoslovakia)
— Laskova, Miss L. (Czechoslovakia)
58 Leand, Miss A. C. (U.S.A.)

— Limmer, Miss J. (Australia)
86 Lindqvist, Miss C. (Sweden)
124 Loosemore, Miss S. J. (Great Britain)
— Ludloff, Miss H. A. (U.S.A.)
— MacGregor, Miss C. (U.S.A.)
— Mager, Mrs. H. L. (U.S.A.)
92 Magers, Mrs. S. W. (U.S.A.)
97 Maleeva, Miss K. (Bulgaria)
20 Maleeva, Miss M. (Bulgaria)
— Maniokova, Miss E. (U.S.S.R.)
44 Martin, Miss S. (U.S.A.)
18 Martinek, Miss V. (Germany)
— May, Miss A. (U.S.A.)
38 McNeil, Miss L. M. (U.S.A.)
78 McQuillan, Miss R. (Australia)
— Melicharova, Miss E. (Czechoslovakia)
43 Minter, Miss A. L. (Australia)
25 Miyagi, Miss N. (Japan)
— Morton, Miss T. J. (Australia)
69 Nagelsen, Miss B. (U.S.A.)
96 Navratilova, Miss M. (U.S.A.)
— Nishiya, Miss A. (Japan)
— Nohacova, Miss A. (Czechoslovakia)
— Novelo, Miss L. (Mexico)
65 Novotna, Miss J. (Czechoslovakia)
56 Oremans, Miss M. (Netherlands)
29 Pampoulova, Miss E. (Bulgaria)
103 Paradis-Mangon, Mrs. P. (France)
116 Paz, Miss M. (Argentina)
— Pfaff, Miss E. S. (Germany)
3 Porwik, Miss C. (Germany)
— Pospisilova, Miss J. (Czechoslovakia)
66 Pratt, Miss N. (Australia)
73 Probst, Miss W. (Germany)
72 Provis, Miss N. (Australia)
126 Quentrec, Miss K. (France)
104 Radford, Miss K. (Australia)
114 Rajchrtova, Miss R. (Czechoslovakia)
105 Rehe, Miss S. C. (U.S.A.)
95 Reinach, Miss E. (South Africa)
68 Reinstadler, Miss B. (Austria)
5 Rinaldi, Miss K. S. (U.S.A.)
34 Rittner, Miss B. (Germany)
35 Romano, Miss F. (Italy)

128 Sabatini, Miss G. (Argentina)
98 Salmon, Miss J. A. (Great Britain)
33 Sanchez Vicario, Miss A. (Spain)
51 Savchenko, Miss L. (U.S.S.R.)
40 Sawamatsu, Miss N. (Japan)
— Scheuer-Larsen, Miss T. (Denmark)
67 Schultz, Miss B. (Netherlands)
— Scott, Miss A. (Australia)
57 Shriver, Miss P. H. (U.S.A.)
83 Sloane, Miss S. P. (U.S.A.)
71 Smith, Miss S. L. (Great Britain)
— Smoller, Miss J. B (U.S.A.)
82 Smylie, Mrs. P. D. (Australia)
— Somerville, Miss B. (U.S.A.)
— Spadea, Miss L. (U.S.A.)
79 Stafford, Miss S. (U.S.A.)
27 Strandlund, Miss M. (Sweden)
123 Strnadova, Miss A. (Czechoslovakia)
125 Stubbs, Miss R. P. (Australia)
84 Suire, Miss C. (France)
48 Sukova, Miss H. (Czechoslovakia)
74 Sviglerova, Miss S. (Czechoslovakia)
113 Tauziat, Miss N. (France)
52 Temesvari, Miss A. (Hungary)
— Ter Riet, Miss H. (Netherlands)
111 Tessi, Miss C. (Argentina)
10 Toleafoa, Miss C. N. (New Zealand)
— Van Buuren, Miss A. (Netherlands)
76 Van Lottum, Miss N. (France)
— Vis, Miss C. M. (Netherlands)
12 Werdel, Miss A. (U.S.A.)
14 White, Miss R. M. (U.S.A.)
19 Whitlinger, Miss T. S. (U.S.A.)
— Whittington, Miss T. (U.S.A.)
— Wibowo, Miss S. (Indonesia)
49 Wiesner, Mrs. H. (Austria)
107 Wood, Miss C. J. (Great Britain)
— Wood, Miss J. (Great Britain)
— Woolcock, Miss A. (Australia)
26 Zardo, Miss S. (Switzerland)
77 Zrubakova, Miss R. (Czechoslovakia)
112 Zvereva, Miss N. (U.S.S.R.)

GENTLEMEN

— Adams, D. (Australia)
— Aerts, N. (Brazil)
65 Agassi, A. (U.S.A.)
6 Aguilera, J. (Spain)
— Albano, P. (Argentina)
110 Altur, J. F. (Spain)
— Amend, E. (U.S.A.)
83 Arraya, P. (Peru)
74 Arrese, J. (Spain)
— Bahrami, M. (Iran)
— Bale, L. J. (South Africa)
109 Bates, M. J. (Great Britain)
— Bathman, R. (Sweden)
3 Baur, P. (Germany)
128 Becker, B. (Germany)
— Beckman, C. (U.S.A.)
— Bergh, R. (Sweden)
120 Bergstrom, C. (Sweden)
— Black, B. (Zimbabwe)
98 Bloom, G. (Israel)
40 Boetsch, A. (France)
— Borwick, N. (Australia)
— Boscatto, M. (Italy)
— Botfield, S. (Great Britain)
— Broad, N. (Great Britain)
— Brown, J. (U.S.A.)
19 Brown, N. (Great Britain)
58 Camporese, O. (Italy)
— Cannon, S. (U.S.A.)
— Canter, J. (U.S.A.)
118 Caratti, C. (Italy)
102 Carbonell, T. (Spain)
22 Cash, P. (Australia)
18 Castle, A. N. (Great Britain)
23 Champion, T. (France)
112 Chang, M. (U.S.A.)
49 Cherkasov, A. (U.S.S.R.)
100 Clavet, F. (Spain)
— Colombini, U. (Italy)
66 Connell, G. (Canada)
25 Connors, J. S. (U.S.A.)
33 Courier, J. (U.S.A.)
44 Curren, K. (U.S.A.)
— Davids, H. (Netherlands)
75 Davis, S. E. (U.S.A.)
— Devries, S. (U.S.A.)
— Doohan, P. (Australia)
39 Dyke, B. (Australia)
— Dzelde, G. (U.S.S.R.)
1 Edberg, S. (Sweden)
78 Eltingh, J. (Netherlands)

95 Evernden, K. (New Zealand)
5 Ferreira, W. (South Africa)
— Fitzgerald, J. B. (Australia)
— Flach, D. (U.S.A.)
— Flach, K. (U.S.A.)
— Flegl, V. (Germany)
12 Fleurian, J. (France)
97 Forget, G. (France)
42 Frana, J. (Argentina)
125 Fromberg, R. (Australia)
— Fulwood, N. A. (Great Britain)
30 Furlan, R. (Italy)
— Galbraith, P. (U.S.A.)
— Garnett, B. (U.S.A.)
— Garrow, B. (U.S.A.)
113 Gilbert, B. (U.S.A.)
34 Gilbert, R. (France)
63 Goldie, D. (U.S.A.)
— Gorriz, M. (Spain)
36 Grabb, J. (U.S.A.)
87 Gunnarsson, J. (Sweden)
99 Gustafsson, M. (Sweden)
70 Haarhuis, P. (Netherlands)
— Hand, P. T. (Great Britain)
— Haygarth, B. (South Africa)
41 Herrera, L. E. (Mexico)
81 Hlasek, J. (Switzerland)
117 Holm, H. (Sweden)
— Ison, D. P. (Great Britain)
17 Ivanisevic, G. (Yugoslavia)
55 Jarryd, A. (Sweden)
124 Jelen, E. (Germany)
— Jensen, L. B. (U.S.A.)
— Jones, K. (U.S.A.)
86 Jonsson, L. (Sweden)
20 Keil, M. (U.S.A.)
— Kinnear, K. (U.S.A.)
93 Koevermans, M. (Netherlands)
92 Korda, P. (Czechoslovakia)
72 Krajicek, R. (Netherlands)
— Kratzmann, A. (Australia)
13 Kratzmann, M. (Australia)
27 Krickstein, A. (U.S.A.)
46 Kriek, J. C. (U.S.A.)
56 Kroon, N. (Sweden)
— Kruger, S. (South Africa)
107 Kuhnen, P. (Germany)
103 Kulti, N. (Sweden)
69 Larsson, M. (Sweden)
52 Laurendeau, M. (Canada)
— Lavalle, L. (Mexico)
90 Layendecker, G. (U.S.A.)

— Leach, R. (U.S.A.)
101 Leconte, H. (France)
96 Lendl, I. (Czechoslovakia)
— Lozano, J. (Mexico)
126 Lundgren, P. (Sweden)
— Luza, G. (Argentina)
— MacPherson, D. (Australia)
116 Mansdorf, A. (Israel)
31 Marcelino, D. (Brazil)
35 Marques, N. (Portugal)
119 Masso, E. (Belgium)
115 Masur, W. (Australia)
121 Matsuoka, S. (Japan)
122 Mattar, L. (Brazil)
111 Mayotte, T. S. (U.S.A.)
16 McEnroe, J. P. (U.S.A.)
79 McEnroe, P. (U.S.A.)
— Melville, S. (U.S.A.)
59 Michibata, G. (Canada)
— Middleton, T. J. (U.S.A.)
— Mora, A. (Venezuela)
— Mordegan, F. (Italy)
— Morgan, J. (Australia)
— Motta, C. (Brazil)
11 Mronz, A. (Germany)
73 Muller, G. (South Africa)
61 Nargiso, D. (Italy)
— Nelson, T. (U.S.A.)
— Nijssen, T. (Netherlands)
— Norval, P. (South Africa)
48 Novacek, K. (Czechoslovakia)
— Nyborg, P. (Sweden)
123 Olhovskiy, A. (U.S.S.R.)
15 Oncins, J. (Brazil)
— Oosting, M. (Netherlands)
114 Orsanic, D. (Argentina)
26 Paloheimo, V. (Finland)
4 Pate, D. (U.S.A.)
— Patridge, S. C. (U.S.A.)
38 Pearce, B. (U.S.A.)
28 Pescosolido, S. (Italy)
105 Petchey, M. R. J. (Great Britain)
89 Pioline, C. (France)
57 Pistolesi, C. (Italy)
37 Pozzi, G. (Italy)
67 Prpic, G. (Yugoslavia)
106 Pugh, J. (U.S.A.)
108 Rahunen, A. (Finland)
9 Raoux, G. (France)
88 Rebolledo, P. (Chile)
50 Reneberg, R. A. (U.S.A.)

47 Riglewski, U. (Germany)
— Rive, J. (U.S.A.)
43 Roese, F. (Brazil)
— Roig, F. (Spain)
2 Rosset, M. (Switzerland)
29 Rostagno, D. (U.S.A.)
71 Ruah, M. (Venezuela)
76 Saceanu, C. (Germany)
— Salumaa, S. (U.S.A.)
32 Sampras, P. (U.S.A.)
80 Sanchez, E. (Spain)
45 Sanchez, J. (Spain)
51 Sapsford, D. E. (Great Britain)
— Schapers, M. (Netherlands)
— Seguso, R. (U.S.A.)
— Shelton, B. (U.S.A.)
68 Siemerink, J. (Netherlands)
10 Skoff, H. (Austria)
— Smid, T. (Czechoslovakia)
— Smith, R. (Bahamas)
127 Steeb, C.-U. (Germany)
64 Stich, M. (Germany)
14 Stolle, S. (Australia)
60 Stoltenberg, J. (Australia)
— Suk, C. (Czechoslovakia)
— Svantesson, T. (Sweden)
— Talbot, B. (South Africa)
21 Tarango, J. (U.S.A.)
— Thorne, K. (U.S.A.)
— Turner, J. M. (Great Britain)
— Vacek, D. (Czechoslovakia)
85 Vajda, M. (Czechoslovakia)
— Van Emburgh, G. (U.S.A.)
7 Van Rensburg, C. J. (South Africa)
— Van't Hof, R. W. (U.S.A.)
— Visser, D. T. (South Africa)
77 Vogel, R. (Czechoslovakia)
54 Volkov, A. (U.S.S.R.)
— Warder, L. (Australia)
94 Washington, M. (U.S.A.)
— Wekesa, P. (Kenya)
91 Wheaton, D. (U.S.A.)
24 Wilkinson, C. (Great Britain)
8 Witsken, T. (U.S.A.)
84 Woodbridge, T. A. (Australia)
62 Woodforde, M. (Australia)
53 Wuyts, B. (Belgium)
— Youl, S. (Australia)
104 Yzaga, J. (Peru)
82 Zivojinovic, S. (Yugoslavia)

144

The Winner will become the holder, for the year only, of the CHALLENGE CUP presented to the Club by KING GEORGE V, and also of the CHALLENGE CUP presented by The All England Lawn Tennis and Croquet Club. The Winner will receive silver replicas of the two Challenge Cups. A Silver Salver will be presented to the Runner-up and a Bronze Medal to each defeated Semi-finalist.

FIRST ROUND	SECOND ROUND	THIRD ROUND	FOURTH ROUND	QUARTER-FINALS	SEMI-FINALS	FINAL
1 **S. Edberg** ① (SWE)	**S. Edberg** ① 6-4, 6-4, 6-4					
2 M. Rosset (SUI)						
3 P. Baur (GER)	D. Pate 4-6, 6-7(7-4), 6-4, 6-2, 6-3	**S. Edberg** ① 6-2, 6-2, 6-3				
4 D. Pate (USA)			**S. Edberg** ① 6-1, 6-3, 6-2			
5 W. Ferreira (RSA)	W. Ferreira 6-4, 6-3, 6-3					
6 J. Aguilera (ESP)		C. J. Van Rensburg 6-4, 7-5, 6-2				
7 C. J. Van Rensburg (RSA)	C. J. Van Rensburg 6-1, 7-6 (7-2), 4-6, 6-4					
8 T. Witsken (USA)				**S. Edberg** ① 7-6 (7-4), 6-1, 6-4		
9 G. Raoux (FRA)	H. Skoff 6-4, 6-4, 6-4					
10 H. Skoff (AUT)		J. Fleurian 6-2, 6-0, 6-3				
11 A. Mronz (GER)	J. Fleurian 6-4, 6-0, 6-3					
12 J. Fleurian (FRA)			J. P. McEnroe ⑯ 6-2, 7-6 (7-4), 6-1			
(Q) 13 M. Kratzmann (AUS)	S. Stolle 6-7 (1-7), 6-3, 5-7 (4-7), 7-6 (9-7), 6-4	J. P. McEnroe ⑯ 7-6 (7-5), 5-7, 6-0, 7-6 (9-7)				
(Q) 14 S. Stolle (AUS)						
15 J. Oncins (BRA)	J. P. McEnroe ⑯ 6-1, 6-2, 6-4					
16 J. P. McEnroe ⑯ (USA)					**S. Edberg** ① 6-3, 6-2, 7-5	
17 G. Ivanisevic ⑩ (YUG)	G. Ivanisevic ⑩ 7-6 (9-7), 6-7 (7-5), 6-2					
(W) 18 A. N. Castle (GBR)		N. Brown 4-6, 6-3, 7-6 (7-3), 6-3				
(W) 19 N. Brown (GBR)	N. Brown 6-4, 7-5, 6-1					
(Q) 20 M. Keil (USA)			T. Champion 7-6 (7-1), 1-6, 7-5, 6-3			
21 J. Tarango (USA)	P. Cash 6-2, 6-3, 6-3	T. Champion 7-5, 6-7 (5-7), 4-6, 6-1, 12-10				
22 P. Cash (AUS)						
23 T. Champion (FRA)	T. Champion 6-4, 6-2, 3-6, 6-4					
(W) 24 C. Wilkinson (GBR)				T. Champion 6-7 (12-14), 6-2, 6-1, 3-6, 6-3		
(W) 25 J. S. Connors (USA)	J. S. Connors 6-2, 6-0, 7-5					
26 V. Paloheimo (FIN)		J. S. Connors 6-3, 6-2, 6-3				
27 A. Krickstein (USA)	A. Krickstein 6-1, 6-3, 6-7 (3-7), 6-7 (8-10), 7-5					
28 S. Pescosolido (ITA)			D. Rostagno 7-6 (7-2), 6-1, 6-4			
29 D. Rostagno (USA)	D. Rostagno 6-0, 6-3, 6-4	D. Rostagno 6-4, 3-6, 7-6 (7-3), 6-4				
30 R. Furlan (ITA)						
(Q) 31 D. Marcelino (BRA)	**P. Sampras** ⑧ 6-1, 6-2, 6-2					
32 **P. Sampras** ⑧ (USA)						**S. Edberg** ① 4-6, 7-6 (7-5), 7-6 (7-5), 7-6 (7-2)
33 **J. Courier** ④ (USA)	**J. Courier** ④ 6-4, 6-2, 7-6 (7-3)					
34 R. Gilbert (FRA)		**J. Courier** ④ 6-4, 7-6 (7-4), 2-6, 4-6, 6-3				
35 N. Marques (POR)	J. Grabb 7-5, 6-7 (5-7), 6-4, 6-1					
36 J. Grabb (USA)			**J. Courier** ④ 6-2, 6-2, 6-0			
(Q) 37 G. Pozzi (ITA)	G. Pozzi 4-6, 6-3, 6-2, 6-2	A. Boetsch 4-6, 7-6 (9-7), 7-6 (9-7), 6-4				
38 B. Pearce (USA)						
(Q) 39 B. Dyke (AUS)	A. Boetsch 6-3, 7-6 (7-3), 6-4					
(Q) 40 A. Boetsch (FRA)				**J. Courier** ④ 6-3, 6-4, 6-2		
41 L. E. Herrera (MEX)	J. Frana 3-6, 2-6, 6-3, 6-3, 6-3					
(Q) 42 J. Frana (ARG)		J. Frana 7-6 (7-4), 6-2, 6-2				
(Q) 43 F. Roese (BRA)	K. Curren 6-3, 6-3, 6-1					
44 K. Curren (USA)			K. Novacek ⑭ 6-0, 6-1, 7-6 (7-2)			
45 J. Sanchez (ESP)	J. Sanchez 6-4, 6-4, 6-7 (5-7), 6-3	K. Novacek ⑭ 6-4, 6-4, 5-7, 6-2				
46 J. C. Kriek (USA)						
(Q) 47 U. Riglewski (GER)	K. Novacek ⑭ 7-6 (7-3), 6-3, 6-4					
48 K. Novacek ⑭ (TCH)					**M. Stich** ⑥ 6-3, 7-6 (7-2), 6-2	
49 A. Cherkasov ⑫ (URS)	R. A. Reneberg 6-4, 6-3, 6-4					
50 R. A. Reneberg (USA)		M. Laurendeau 3-6, 6-4, 6-7 (4-7), 6-4, 6-2				
(W) 51 D. E. Sapsford (GBR)	M. Laurendeau 6-3, 7-6 (7-4), 6-7 (4-7), 6-4, 6-2					
(L) 52 M. Laurendeau (CAN)			A. Volkov 6-2, 3-6, 6-3, 3-6, 8-6			
53 B. Wuyts (BEL)	A. Volkov 6-1, 6-2, 6-2	A. Volkov 6-2, 6-3, 6-4, 3-6, 8-6				
54 A. Volkov (URS)						
55 A. Jarryd (SWE)	A. Jarryd 6-3, 6-4, 3-6, 6-3					
(L) 56 N. Kroon (SWE)				A. Volkov 6-1, 6-2, 6-1		
57 C. Pistolesi (ITA)	O. Camporese 6-1, 6-3, 2-6, 6-3					
58 O. Camporese (ITA)		O. Camporese 7-5, 6-2, 6-1				
(Q) 59 G. Michibata (CAN)	G. Michibata 5-7, 6-4, 3-6, 7-6 (7-4), 6-4					
60 J. Stoltenberg (AUS)			**M. Stich** ⑥ 7-6 (7-0), 6-2, 6-7, (4-7), 6-4			
(L) 61 D. Nargiso (ITA)	D. Nargiso 6-4, 7-6 (9-7), 7-6 (7-3)	**M. Stich** ⑥ 6-3, 6-4, 6-7 (5-7), 6-2				
62 M. Woodforde (AUS)						
63 D. Goldie (USA)	**M. Stich** ⑥ 6-4, 6-1, 6-2					
64 **M. Stich** ⑥ (GER)				**M. Stich** ⑥ 4-6, 6-3, 7-5, 1-6, 7-5		
65 **A. Agassi** ⑤ (USA)	**A. Agassi** ⑤ 4-6, 6-1, 6-7 (6-8), 7-5, 6-3					
66 G. Connell (CAN)		**A. Agassi** ⑤ 7-6 (7-3), 3-6, 6-4, 6-2				
67 G. Prpic (YUG)	G. Prpic 6-4, 3-6, 6-3, 3-6, 10-8					
68 J. Siemerink (HOL)			**A. Agassi** ⑤ 7-6 (7-5), 6-3, 7-6 (7-2)			
69 M. Larsson (SWE)	M. Larsson 6-4, 1-6, 6-3, 6-1	R. Krajicek 6-3, 6-4, 6-3				
70 P. Haarhuis (HOL)						
(L) 71 M. Ruah (VEN)	R. Krajicek 5-7, 6-1, 3-6, 6-3, 6-4					
72 R. Krajicek (HOL)				**A. Agassi** ⑤ 6-3, 3-6, 6-3, 6-4		
73 G. Muller (RSA)	G. Muller 6-2, 6-3, 6-3					
74 J. Arrese (ESP)		C. Saceanu 7-6 (8-6), 6-4, 3-6, 7-6 (7-5)				
75 S. E. Davis (USA)	C. Saceanu 6-4, 7-6 (7-3), 6-4					
76 C. Saceanu (GER)			J. Eltingh 7-6 (7-5), 2-6, 1-6, 6-4, 12-10			
(Q) 77 R. Vogel (TCH)	J. Eltingh 7-6 (7-2), 6-7 (6-8), 7-6 (7-5), 6-7 (7-9), 6-3	J. Eltingh 6-3, 4-6, 6-4, 7-5				
78 J. Eltingh (HOL)						
79 P. McEnroe (USA)	P. McEnroe 6-3, 7-6 (7-4), 6-1					
80 **E. Sanchez** ⑪ (ESP)				J. Eltingh 6-3, 4-6, 6-4, 7-5		
81 **J. Hlasek** (SUI)	**J. Hlasek** 6-2, 3-6, 6-3, 6-2					
(Q) 82 S. Zivojinovic (YUG)		T. A. Woodbridge 6-3, 1-6, 7-5, 6-3				
83 P. Arraya (PER)	T. A. Woodbridge 2-6, 6-2, 6-3, 6-1					
84 T. A. Woodbridge (AUS)			J. Gunnarsson 7-6 (7-4), 4-6, 6-3, 6-4			
85 M. Vajda (TCH)	L. Jonsson 7-5, 6-3, 7-5	J. Gunnarsson 6-2, 6-3, 2-6, 7-6 (7-4)				
86 L. Jonsson (SWE)						
87 J. Gunnarsson (SWE)	J. Gunnarsson 6-1, 7-5, 6-2					
88 P. Rebolledo (CHI)				D. Wheaton 6-4, 6-3, 6-1		
89 C. Pioline (FRA)	C. Pioline 4-6, 4-6, 3-6, 6-4, 7-6 (7-4)					
(Q) 90 G. Layendecker (USA)		D. Wheaton 6-4, 6-7 (5-7), 6-3, 6-3				
91 D. Wheaton (USA)	D. Wheaton 7-6 (7-4), 6-7 (6-8), 6-4, 6-2					
92 P. Korda (TCH)			I. Lendl ③ 4-6, 2-6, 6-4, 6-4, 7-5			
93 M. Koevermans (HOL)	M. Washington 6-3, 6-2, 6-1	I. Lendl ③ 6-2, 7-5, 7-6 (7-5)				
94 M. Washington (USA)						
95 K. Evernden (NZL)	I. Lendl ③ 6-2, 7-5, 7-6 (7-5)					
96 I. Lendl ③ (TCH)				D. Wheaton ② 6-4, 7-6 (7-4), 7-5		
97 **G. Forget** ⑦ (FRA)	**G. Forget** ⑦ 6-2, 7-6 (7-2), 7-5, 6-7 (4-7), 6-4					
98 G. Bloom (ISR)		**G. Forget** ⑦ 6-4, 6-3, 6-4				
99 M. Gustafsson (SWE)	M. Gustafsson 7-6 (7-5), 6-3, 6-3					
100 F. Clavet (ESP)			**G. Forget** ⑦ 3-6, 4-6, 6-1, 4-1 Ret'd.			
101 H. Leconte (FRA)	H. Leconte 6-3, 6-1, 7-6 (7-2)	H. Leconte 6-4, 6-2, 6-3				
102 T. Carbonell (ESP)						
103 N. Kulti (SWE)	J. Yzaga 6-2, 7-5, 5-7, 6-1					
104 J. Yzaga (PER)				**G. Forget** ⑦ 6-7 (4-7), 7-5, 6-2, 6-4		
(W) 105 M. R. J. Petchey (GBR)	M. R. J. Petchey 4-6, 4-6, 6-3, 6-3, 8-6					
(W) 106 J. Pugh (USA)		P. Kuhnen 6-2, 6-4, 6-3				
107 P. Kuhnen (GER)	P. Kuhnen 6-2, 6-4, 6-2					
108 A. Rahunen (FIN)			T. S. Mayotte 3-6, 6-2, 7-6 (7-4), 6-4			
(W) 109 M. J. Bates (GBR)	M. J. Bates 6-4, 6-4, 6-2	T. S. Mayotte 6-3, 3-6, 6-4, 7-6 (7-2)				
110 J. F. Altur (ESP)						
111 T. S. Mayotte (USA)	T. S. Mayotte 6-7 (6-8), 4-6, 7-6 (11-9), 6-2					
112 **M. Chang** ⑨ (USA)				B. Becker ② 6-4, 7-6 (7-4), 7-5		
113 **B. Gilbert** ⑮ (USA)	**B. Gilbert** ⑮ 7-5, 6-1, 6-2					
(Q) 114 D. Orsanic (ARG)		**B. Gilbert** ⑮ 7-5, 2-6, 6-3, 5-7, 6-4				
115 W. Masur (AUS)	W. Masur 6-3, 1-6, 7-6 (7-3), 6-4					
116 A. Mansdorf (ISR)			C. Bergstrom 6-3, 6-2, 3-6, 6-3			
(Q) 117 H. Holm (SWE)	H. Holm 7-6 (7-3), 6-3, 6-4	C. Bergstrom 7-5, 6-0, 6-4				
118 C. Caratti (ITA)						
119 E. Masso (BEL)	C. Bergstrom 6-1, 7-5, 6-3					
120 C. Bergstrom (SWE)				B. Becker ② 6-4, 6-7 (4-7), 6-1, 7-6 (7-2)		
121 S. Matsuoka (JPN)	L. Mattar 6-4, 4-6, 6-7 (8-10), 7-5, 7-5					
122 L. Mattar (BRA)		A. Olhovskiy 2-6, 7-6 (7-3), 6-4, 4-6, 6-3				
(L) 123 A. Olhovskiy (URS)	A. Olhovskiy 3-6, 6-3, 6-3, 7-6 (7-4)					
124 E. Jelen (GER)			B. Becker ② 6-1, 6-4, 3-6, 6-3			
125 R. Fromberg (AUS)	P. Lundgren 6-4, 7-6 (8-6), 6-2	**B. Becker** ② 7-6 (7-3), 7-5, 7-5				
126 P. Lundgren (SWE)						
127 C.-U. Steeb (GER)	**B. Becker** ② 6-4, 6-2, 6-4					
128 **B. Becker** ② (GER)						

Quarter-finals / Semi-finals / Final summary:

S. Edberg ① 7-6 (7-4), 6-1, 6-4
T. Champion 6-7 (12-14), 6-2, 6-1, 3-6, 6-3
J. Courier ④ 6-3, 6-4, 6-2
M. Stich ⑥ 4-6, 6-3, 7-5, 1-6, 7-5
A. Agassi ⑤ 6-3, 3-6, 6-3, 6-4
D. Wheaton 6-4, 6-3, 6-1
G. Forget ⑦ 6-7 (4-7), 7-5, 6-2, 6-4
B. Becker ② 6-4, 6-7 (4-7), 6-1, 7-6 (7-2)

Semi-finals:
S. Edberg ① 6-3, 6-2, 7-5
M. Stich ⑥ 6-3, 7-6 (7-2), 6-2
D. Wheaton ② 6-4, 7-6 (7-4), 7-5
B. Becker ② 6-7 (5-7), 7-6 (7-3), 6-2, 6-7, (9-7)

Final:
M. Stich ⑥ 6-4, 7-6 (7-4), 6-4

Heavy type denotes seeded players. The encircled figure against names denotes the order in which they have been seeded. (W) = Wild card. (Q) = Qualifier. (L) = Lucky loser. The Matches will be the best of five sets.

145

EVENT II.—THE GENTLEMEN'S DOUBLES CHAMPIONSHIP

Holders: R. LEACH and J. PUGH

The Winners will become the holders, for the year only, of the CHALLENGE CUPS, presented by the OXFORD UNIVERSITY LAWN TENNIS CLUB and the late SIR HERBERT WILBERFORCE respectively. The Winners will receive silver replicas of the Challenge Cups. A Silver Salver will be presented to each of the Runners-up and a Bronze Medal to each defeated Semi-finalist.

FIRST ROUND

1	**S. E. Davis and D. Pate** ①
2	A. Mora and T. Svantesson
3	V. Flegl and G. Prpic
(Q) 4	H. Holm and P. Nyborg
(W) 5	S. Botfield and J. M. Turner
6	H. Davids and J. Siemerink
7	M. Oosting and P. Wekesa
8	**W. Ferreira and P. Norval** ⑤
9	**U. Riglewski and M. Stich** ⑨
(Q) 10	B. Haygarth and B. Talbot
11	S. Devries and D. MacPherson
12	L. Mattar and J. Oncins
13	S. C. Patridge and J. Rive
(W) 14	D. P. Ison and M. R. J. Petchey
15	F. Mordegan and R. Vogel
16	**T. A. Woodbridge and M. Woodforde** ⑧
17	**R. Leach and J. Pugh** ③
(W) 18	G. Ivanisevic and J. P. McEnroe
19	J. Courier and D. Flach
20	A. Olhovskiy and L. Pimek
21	P. Annacone and K. Evernden
22	K. Novacek and T. Smid
(Q) 23	B. Black and T. J. Middleton
24	**J. Grabb and P. McEnroe** ⑥
25	**P. Haarhuis and M. Koevermans** ⑫
26	M. Schapers and R. Smith
27	G. Layendecker and R. A. Reneberg
28	T. Nelson and B. Shelton
29	M. Gorriz and F. Roig
30	J. Frana and L. Lavalle
31	N. Aerts and R. W. Van't Hof
32	**G. Muller and D. T. Visser** ⑬
(L) 33	D. Adams and G. Dzelde
34	K. Kinnear and S. Salumaa
35	J. Brown and B. Garnett
36	M. Boscatto and S. Pescosolido
37	P. Albano and S. Cannon
38	D. Nargiso and J. Sanchez
39	M. J. Bates and N. Brown
40	**K. Jones and J. Lozano** ⑪
41	**N. Broad and K. Curren** ⑭
42	R. Krajicek and D. Vacek
43	K. Flach and R. Seguso
44	R. Bathman and R. Bergh
45	T. Carbonell and P. Korda
46	C. Beckman and S. Melville
47	A. N. Castle and G. Van Emburgh
48	**G. Connell and G. Michibata** ④
49	**P. Galbraith and T. Witsken** ⑦
50	M. Bahrami and R. Gilbert
51	S. Kruger and C. J. Van Rensburg
52	B. Garrow and B. Pearce
53	T. Nijssen and C. Suk
(Q) 54	M. Laurendeau and F. Roese
55	G. Bloom and P. Doohan
56	**L. B. Jensen and L. Warder** ⑩
57	**B. Dyke and P. Lundgren** ⑯
(W) 58	N. A. Fulwood and D. E. Sapsford
(W) 59	P. T. Hand and C. Wilkinson
60	M. Kratzmann and S. Youl
(Q) 61	N. Borwick and A. Kratzmann
62	G. Luza and C. Motta
63	W. Masur and J. Stoltenberg
64	**J. B. Fitzgerald and A. Jarryd** ②

SECOND ROUND

S. E. Davis and D. Pate ①	6-4, 6-4
H. Holm and P. Nyborg	6-2, 6-3
S. Botfield and J. M. Turner	7-6 (7-4), 7-6 (7-4)
W. Ferreira and P. Norval ⑤	7-6 (7-5), 7-5
B. Haygarth and B. Talbot	7-6 (7-4), 6-3
S. Devries and D. MacPherson	6-3, 7-5
S. C. Patridge and J. Rive	3-6, 6-3, 6-4
T. A. Woodbridge and M. Woodforde ⑧	6-4, 6-3
G. Ivanisevic and J. P. McEnroe	6-3, 6-4
J. Courier and D. Flach	6-3, 6-3
P. Annacone and K. Evernden	6-7 (5-7), 7-6 (7-5), 6-3
B. Black and T. J. Middleton	3-6, 6-3, 6-3
P. Haarhuis and M. Koevermans ⑫	6-1, 7-6 (7-0)
G. Layendecker and R. A. Reneberg	6-2, 5-7, 6-2
J. Frana and L. Lavalle	6-2, 6-2
G. Muller and D. T. Visser ⑬	6-3, 6-4
D. Adams and G. Dzelde	6-3, 6-4
J. Brown and B. Garnett	6-3, 6-7 (6-8), 6-4
P. Albano and S. Cannon	3-6, 6-3, 6-4
K. Jones and J. Lozano ⑪	6-3, 7-5
R. Krajicek and D. Vacek	6-4, 6-3
K. Flach and R. Seguso	7-6 (7-3), 6-4
T. Carbonell and P. Korda	6-2, 6-4
G. Connell and G. Michibata ④	6-4, 6-2
P. Galbraith and T. Witsken ⑦	7-5, 6-3
B. Garrow and B. Pearce	6-3, 6-3
T. Nijssen and C. Suk	6-4, 6-4
L. B. Jensen and L. Warder ⑩	6-4, 6-4
N. A. Fulwood and D. E. Sapsford	6-4, 6-4
M. Kratzmann and S. Youl	7-6 (7-4), 6-3
G. Luza and C. Motta	6-1, 6-2
J. B. Fitzgerald and A. Jarryd ②	6-3, 6-4

THIRD ROUND

S. E. Davis and D. Pate ①	6-3, 7-6 (7-2)
W. Ferreira and P. Norval ⑤	7-5, 6-3
B. Haygarth and B. Talbot	6-4, 6-4
T. A. Woodbridge and M. Woodforde ⑧	4-6, 6-4
J. Courier and D. Flach	3-6, 7-6 (7-2), 6-4
P. Annacone and K. Evernden	6-3, 7-5
P. Haarhuis and M. Koevermans ⑫	7-6 (9-7), 6-3
J. Frana and L. Lavalle	7-6 (8-6), 6-3
J. Brown and B. Garnett	7-6 (7-5), 6-4
P. Albano and S. Cannon	6-3, 6-3
K. Flach and R. Seguso	7-6 (8-6), 6-3
G. Connell and G. Michibata ④	6-4, 7-5
P. Galbraith and T. Witsken ⑦	6-7 (2-7), 6-4, 6-3
T. Nijssen and C. Suk	7-5, 3-6, 7-5
M. Kratzmann and S. Youl	6-3, 6-4
J. B. Fitzgerald and A. Jarryd ②	6-4, 7-6 (7-4)

QUARTER-FINALS

W. Ferreira and P. Norval ⑤	7-6 (7-2), 5-7, 9-7
T. A. Woodbridge and M. Woodforde ⑧	6-2, 6-3
P. Annacone and K. Evernden	6-2, 7-6 (7-2)
J. Frana and L. Lavalle	6-3, 6-4
P. Albano and S. Cannon	7-6 (7-3), 6-3
G. Connell and G. Michibata ④	6-4, 7-6 (7-0)
P. Galbraith and T. Witsken ⑦	6-4, 4-6, 13-11
J. B. Fitzgerald and A. Jarryd ②	7-6 (7-3), 6-4

SEMI-FINALS

W. Ferreira and P. Norval ⑤	7-6 (7-3), 6-4, 6-4
J. Frana and L. Lavalle	6-2, 6-4, 7-5
G. Connell and G. Michibata ④	5-7, 2-6, 7-6 (7-5), 7-6 (11-9), 10-8
J. B. Fitzgerald and A. Jarryd ②	6-2, 6-7 (4-7), 7-6 (7-5), 6-4

FINAL

J. Frana and L. Lavalle	6-2, 6-4, 6-7 (7-9), 7-4
J. B. Fitzgerald and A. Jarryd ②	

Winner: J. B. Fitzgerald and A. Jarryd ② 6-3, 6-4, 6-7 (7-9), 6-1

Heavy type denotes seeded players. The encircled figure against names denotes the order in which they have been seeded. (W) = Wild card. (Q) = Qualifier. (L) = Lucky loser. The Matches will be the best of five sets.

EVENT III.—THE LADIES' SINGLES CHAMPIONSHIP

Holder: Miss M. NAVRATILOVA

The Winner will become the holder, for the year only, of the CHALLENGE TROPHY presented by The All England Lawn Tennis and Croquet Club. The Winner will receive a silver replica of the Trophy. A Silver Salver will be presented to the Runner-up and a Bronze Medal to each defeated Semi-finalist.

FIRST ROUND

1	**Miss S. Graf** ①	(GER)
2	Miss S. Appelmans	(BEL)
3	Miss C. Porwik	(GER)
4	Mrs. T. A. Harper	(USA)
5	Miss K. S. Rinaldi	(USA)
6	Miss N. Herreman	(FRA)
7	Miss A. B. Henricksson	(USA)
8	Miss Y. Basuki	(INA)
9	Miss J. Halard	(FRA)
(L) 10	Miss C. N. Toleafoa	(NZL)
11	Miss D. A. Graham	(USA)
12	Miss M. Werdel	(USA)
13	Miss F. Bonsignori	(ITA)
14	Miss R. M. White	(USA)
15	Miss K. Kschwendt	(LUX)
16	**Miss A. Frazier** ⑭	(USA)
17	**Miss A. Huber** ⑬	(GER)
18	Miss V. Martinek	(GER)
19	Miss T. S. Whitlinger	(USA)
20	Miss M. Maleeva	(BUL)
21	Miss M. M. Bollegraf	(HOL)
(W) 22	Miss V.S. Humphreys-Davies	(GBR)
23	Miss J. M. Durie	(GBR)
24	Miss H. Kelesi	(CAN)
25	Miss N. Miyagi	(JPN)
26	Miss E. Zardo	(SUI)
27	Miss M. Strandlund	(SWE)
28	Miss R. Hiraki	(JPN)
29	Miss E. Pampoulova	(BUL)
(W) 30	Miss B. A. Borneo	(GBR)
31	Miss S. L. Gomer	(GBR)
32	**Miss Z. L. Garrison** ⑦	(USA)
33	**Miss A. Sanchez Vicario** ④	(ESP)
34	Miss B. Rittner	(GER)
35	Miss F. Romano	(ITA)
36	Miss A. J. Coetzer	(RSA)
37	Miss P. Langrova	(TCH)
38	Miss L. M. McNeil	(USA)
39	Miss C. Bartos	(SUI)
40	Miss N. Sawamatsu	(JPN)
(L) 41	Miss J.-A. Faull	(AUS)
42	Miss K. Godridge	(AUS)
43	Miss A. L. Minter	(AUS)
44	Miss S. Martin	(USA)
45	Miss D. L. Faber	(USA)
46	Miss C. Caverzasio	(SUI)
47	Miss G. Fernandez	(PUR)
48	**Miss H. Sukova** ⑩	(TCH)
49	**Mrs. H. Wiesner** ⑯	(AUT)
50	Miss H. Cioffi	(USA)
51	Miss L. Savchenko	(URS)
52	Miss A. Temesvari	(HUN)
(W) 53	Miss B. Griffiths	(GBR)
54	Miss C. Kohde-Kilsch	(GER)
(Q) 55	Miss N. A. M. Jagerman	(HOL)
(Q) 56	Miss M. Oremans	(HOL)
57	Miss P. H. Shriver	(USA)
58	Miss A. C. Leand	(USA)
59	Miss E. De Lone	(USA)
60	Miss B. Fulco	(ARG)
61	Miss A. A. Keller	(USA)
62	Miss L. Golarsa	(ITA)
(Q) 63	Miss P. Kamstra	(HOL)
64	**Miss M. J. Fernandez** ⑤	(USA)
65	**Miss J. Novotna** ⑥	(TCH)
(L) 66	Miss N. Pratt	(AUS)
67	Miss B. Schultz	(HOL)
68	Miss B. Reinstadler	(AUT)
69	Miss B. Nagelsen	(USA)
70	Miss E. Brioukhovets	(URS)
71	Miss S. L. Smith	(GBR)
72	Miss N. Provis	(AUS)
73	Miss W. Probst	(GER)
74	Miss E. Sviglerova	(TCH)
(Q) 75	Miss E. Callens	(BEL)
76	Miss N. Van Lottum	(FRA)
77	Miss R. Zrubakova	(TCH)
78	Miss R. McQuillan	(AUS)
79	Miss S. C. Stafford	(USA)
80	**Miss J. Capriati** ⑨	(USA)
81	**Miss A. M. Cecchini** ⑮	(ITA)
82	Mrs. P. D. Smylie	(AUS)
83	Miss S. P. Sloane	(USA)
(Q) 84	Miss C. Suire	(FRA)
(Q) 85	Miss I. Demongeot	(FRA)
86	Miss C. Lindqvist	(SWE)
87	Miss K. Habsudova	(TCH)
88	Miss C. Dahlman	(SWE)
(W) 89	Miss S. L. Bentley	(GBR)
90	Miss M. Kidowaki	(JPN)
91	Miss L. Garrone	(ITA)
92	Mrs. S. W. Magers	(USA)
93	Miss A. Dechaume	(FRA)
(W) 94	Miss A. L. Grunfeld	(GBR)
95	Miss E. Reinach	(RSA)
96	**Miss M. Navratilova** ③	(USA)
97	**Miss K. Maleeva** ⑧	(BUL)
98	Miss J. A. Salmon	(GBR)
(W) 99	Miss K. D. Hand	(GBR)
100	Miss A. Grossman	(USA)
101	Mrs. R.D. Fairbank-Nideffer	(USA)
102	Miss P. Hy	(CAN)
103	Mrs. P. Paradis-Mangon	(FRA)
(Q) 104	Miss K. Radford	(AUS)
105	Miss S. C. Rehe	(USA)
106	Miss M. De Swardt	(RSA)
107	Miss C. J. Wood	(GBR)
108	Mrs. L. Gildemeister	(PER)
109	Miss L. M. Harvey-Wild	(USA)
110	Mrs. T. J. Kreiss	(USA)
111	Miss C. Tessi	(ARG)
112	**Miss N. Zvereva** ⑫	(URS)
113	**Miss N. Tauziat** ⑪	(FRA)
114	Miss R. Rajchrtova	(TCH)
115	Miss A. Kijimuta	(JPN)
116	Miss M. Paz	(ARG)
(L) 117	Miss J. M. Hetherington	(CAN)
118	Miss P. A. Fendick	(USA)
119	Miss L. Ferrando	(ITA)
(L) 120	Miss K. Date	(JPN)
121	Miss G. Helgeson	(USA)
122	Miss C. E. Cunningham	(USA)
123	Miss A. Strnadova	(TCH)
(W) 124	Miss S. J. Loosemore	(GBR)
(Q) 125	Miss R. P. Stubbs	(AUS)
126	Miss K. Quentrec	(FRA)
127	Miss M. Javer	(GBR)
128	**Miss G. Sabatini** ②	(ARG)

SECOND ROUND

- Miss S. Graf ① — 6-2, 6-2
- Mrs. T. A. Harper — 6-4, 6-1
- Miss N. Herreman — 7-5, 6-2
- Miss Y. Basuki — 6-4, 7-6, (7-4)
- Miss J. Halard — 6-1, 2-6, 6-3
- Miss M. Werdel — 6-3, 6-2
- Miss R. M. White — 6-1, 6-1
- Miss A. Frazier ⑭ — 7-6 (7-3), 6-4
- Miss A. Huber ⑬ — 6-1, 6-2
- Miss T. S. Whitlinger — 6-1, 6-3
- Miss M. M. Bollegraf — 6-4, 6-4
- Miss J. M. Durie — 6-3, 6-2
- Miss E. Zardo — 6-0, 6-3
- Miss M. Strandlund — 6-2, 7-6(7-5)
- Miss E. Pampoulova — 2-6, 6-3, 6-4
- Miss Z. L. Garrison ⑦ — 6-3, 6-3
- Miss A. Sanchez Vicario ④ — 6-1, 6-2
- Miss A. J. Coetzer — 7-6(7-5), 6-2
- Miss L. M. McNeil — 6-4, 7-5
- Miss N. Sawamatsu — 6-2, 6-2
- Miss J.-A. Faull — 6-0, 6-2
- Miss A. L. Minter — 6-4, 6-0
- Miss D. L. Faber — 6-3, 6-7 (4-7), 6-2
- Miss G. Fernandez — 4-6, 6-1, 6-4
- Mrs. H. Wiesner ⑯ — 6-1, 6-2
- Miss L. Savchenko — 6-2, 6-7 (5-7), 8-6
- Miss C. Kohde-Kilsch — 6-1, 6-3
- Miss N. A. M. Jagerman — 7-5, 6-4
- Miss P. H. Shriver — 6-0, 7-5
- Miss B. Fulco — 3-6, 6-2, 6-4
- Miss A. A. Keller
- Miss M. J. Fernandez ⑤ — 6-2, 6-4
- Miss J. Novotna ⑥ — 6-3, 6-0
- Miss B. Schultz — 6-3, 6-0
- Miss E. Brioukhovets — 6-2, 6-1
- Miss N. Provis — 3-6, 6-4, 6-2
- Miss W. Probst — 7-6 (8-6), 7-5
- Miss E. Callens — 7-6 (7-1), 2-6, 7-5
- Miss R. Zrubakova — 7-6 (7-4), 6-2
- Miss J. Capriati ⑨ — 6-0, 7-5
- Mrs. P. D. Smylie — 6-3, 6-4
- Miss C. Suire — 6-2, 6-2
- Miss C. Lindqvist — 6-1, 6-0
- Miss K. Habsudova — 6-3, 6-2
- Miss M. Kidowaki — 1-6, 7-5, 6-1
- Miss L. Garrone — 6-4, 7-6 (7-5)
- Miss A. L. Grunfeld — 6-4, 6-4
- Miss M. Navratilova ③ — 4-6, 6-2, 6-4
- Miss K. Maleeva ⑧ — 7-5, 6-3
- Miss A. Grossman
- Miss P. Hy — 6-2, 3-6, 6-0
- Mrs. P. Paradis-Mangon — 6-3, 6-2
- Miss M. De Swardt — 6-3, 3-6, 6-4
- Mrs. L. Gildemeister — 6-4, 6-4
- Miss L. M. Harvey-Wild — 6-4, 6-2
- Miss N. Zvereva ⑫ — 7-6 (7-3), 6-4
- Miss N. Tauziat ⑪ — 6-4, 7-5
- Miss A. Kijimuta — 6-1, 6-3
- Miss P. A. Fendick — 7-6 (7-5), 4-6, 6-1
- Miss L. Ferrando — 6-4, 3-6, 6-2
- Miss C. E. Cunningham — 7-6 (14-12), 6-4
- Miss A. Strnadova — 6-4, 7-5
- Miss K. Quentrec — 6-2, 6-2
- Miss G. Sabatini ② — 6-4, 6-0

THIRD ROUND

- Miss S. Graf ① — 6-0, 6-1
- Miss Y. Basuki — 6-4, 6-4
- Miss M. Werdel — 6-2, 6-4
- Miss A. Frazier ⑭ — 7-5, 6-4
- Miss A. Huber ⑬ — 6-2, 6-1
- Miss M. M. Bollegraf — 6-3, 5-7, 6-3
- Miss M. Strandlund — 6-4, 6-4
- Miss Z. L. Garrison ⑦ — 6-3, 6-1
- Miss A. Sanchez Vicario ④ — 6-4, 6-1
- Miss L. M. McNeil — 3-6, 6-2, 6-2
- Miss A. L. Minter — 6-3, 6-2
- Miss G. Fernandez — 7-5, 7-5
- Mrs. H. Wiesner ⑯ — 6-3, 6-0
- Miss C. Kohde-Kilsch — 7-6 (7-2), 6-2
- Miss P. H. Shriver — 6-0, 6-3
- Miss M. J. Fernandez ⑤ — 7-6 (7-5), 6-1
- Miss B. Schultz — 4-6, 7-6 (7-5), 6-4
- Miss E. Brioukhovets — 7-6 (7-3), 6-4
- Miss W. Probst — 7-6 (7-5), 6-3
- Miss J. Capriati ⑨ — 6-2, 6-3
- Mrs. P. D. Smylie — 6-3, 6-4
- Miss C. Lindqvist — 6-3, 6-2
- Miss L. Garrone — 6-4, 6-3
- Miss M. Navratilova ③ — 6-3, 6-1
- Miss K. Maleeva ⑧ — 6-4, 6-4
- Miss P. Hy — 4-6, 6-4, 6-2
- Mrs. L. Gildemeister — 6-4, 6-1
- Miss L. M. Harvey-Wild — 6-4, 6-1
- Miss N. Tauziat ⑪ — 3-6, 6-2, 6-2
- Miss L. Ferrando — 4-6, 6-1, 7-5
- Miss A. Strnadova — 6-1, 6-3
- Miss G. Sabatini ② — 6-4, 6-2

FOURTH ROUND

- Miss S. Graf ① — 6-2, 6-3
- Miss A. Frazier ⑭ — 6-2, 6-1
- Miss A. Huber ⑬ — 6-3, 6-7 (5-7), 6-0
- Miss Z. L. Garrison ⑦ — 6-3, 6-3
- Miss A. Sanchez Vicario ④ — 6-2, 6-4
- Miss A. L. Minter — 6-3, 6-3
- Mrs. H. Wiesner ⑯ — 3-6, 7-5, 6-1
- Miss M. J. Fernandez ⑤ — 6-3, 7-5
- Miss B. Schultz — 5-7, 6-4, 7-5
- Miss J. Capriati ⑨ — 6-3, 1-6, 6-3
- Miss C. Lindqvist — 6-1, 7-6 (7-5)
- Miss M. Navratilova ③ — 6-2, 6-2
- Miss K. Maleeva ⑧ — 6-3, 6-4
- Mrs. L. Gildemeister — 2-2 Retired
- Miss N. Tauziat ⑪ — 6-1, 6-1
- Miss G. Sabatini ② — 6-1, 6-3

QUARTER-FINALS

- Miss S. Graf ① — 6-2, 6-1
- Miss Z. L. Garrison ⑦ — 4-6, 6-3, 6-0
- Miss A. Sanchez Vicario ④ — 7-5, 3-6, 6-1
- Miss M. J. Fernandez ⑤ — 6-0, 7-5
- Miss J. Capriati ⑨ — 3-6, 6-1, 6-1
- Miss M. Navratilova ③ — 6-1, 6-3
- Mrs. L. Gildemeister — 3-6, 6-2, 6-3
- Miss G. Sabatini ② — 7-6 (7-3), 6-3

SEMI-FINALS

- Miss S. Graf ① — 6-1, 6-3
- Miss M. J. Fernandez ⑤ — 6-2, 7-5
- Miss J. Capriati ⑨ — 6-4, 7-5
- Miss G. Sabatini ② — 6-2, 6-1

FINAL

- Miss S. Graf ① — 6-2, 6-4
- Miss G. Sabatini ② — 6-4, 6-4

Champion: Miss S. Graf ① — 6-4, 3-6, 8-6

Heavy type denotes seeded players. The encircled figure against names denotes the order in which they have been seeded. (W) = Wild card. (Q) = Qualifier. (L) = Lucky loser. The Matches will be the best of three sets.

147

EVENT IV.—THE LADIES' DOUBLES CHAMPIONSHIP

Holders: Miss J. NOVOTNA and Miss H. SUKOVA

The Winners will become the holders, for the year, of the CHALLENGE CUP presented by H.R.H. PRINCESS MARINA, DUCHESS OF KENT, the late President of The All England Lawn Tennis and Croquet Club. The Winners will receive silver replicas of the Challenge Cup. A Silver Salver will be presented to each of the Runners-up and a Bronze Medal to each defeated Semi-finalist.

FIRST ROUND

1 **Miss G. Fernandez and Miss J. Novotna** ①
2 Miss P. Langrova and Miss R. Zrubakova
3 Miss S. C. Rehe and Miss A. Temesvari
4 Miss K. Maleeva and Miss M. Maleeva
(W) 5 Miss A. L. Grunfeld and Miss S. J. Loosemore
(Q) 6 Miss B. Griffiths and Miss J. Wood
7 Miss N. Jankovska and Miss E. Melicharova
8 **Miss J. M. Hetherington and Miss K. S. Rinaldi** ⑫
9 **Miss E. M. Burgin and Miss P. A. Fendick** ⑨
10 Miss S. C. Stafford and Miss T. S. Whitlinger
11 Miss B. A. Borneo and Miss C. J. Wood
12 Miss C. Bakkum and Miss N. A. M. Jagerman
13 Miss E. S. Pfaff and Miss R. P. Stubbs
14 Miss Y. Basuki and Miss S. Wibowo
15 Miss I. Demongeot and Miss J. M. Durie
16 **Mrs. S. W. Magers and Miss R. M. White** ⑦
17 **Miss M. J. Fernandez and Miss Z. L. Garrison** ④
18 Miss L. Laskova and Miss E. Maniokova
(L) 19 Miss L. Novelo and Miss B. Somerville
20 Miss G. E. Coorengel and Miss A. Van Buuren
(Q) 21 Miss R. Hiraki and Miss A. Nishiya
22 Miss M. Jaggard and Miss C. Suire
23 Miss H. Kelesi and Miss J. B. Smoller
24 **Miss C. Kohde-Kilsch and Miss E. Reinach** ③
25 **Miss L. J. Gregory and Miss A. May** ⑯
26 Miss A. Kijimuta and Miss N. Miyagi
(Q) 27 Miss C. Benjamin and Miss T. Whittington
28 Miss R. Rajchrtova and Miss A. Strnadova
29 Miss P. Paradis-Mangon and Miss A. Scott
30 Miss L. Ferrando and Miss L. Golarsa
31 Miss A. Dechaume and Miss W. Probst
32 **Miss K. Jordan and Miss L. M. McNeil** ⑤
33 **Miss M. Navratilova and Miss P. H. Shriver** ⑧
(W) 34 Miss K. D. Hand and Miss J. A. Salmon
(W) 35 Miss S. L. Gomer and Miss V. Lake
36 Miss T. A. Harper and Miss M. Kidowaki
37 Miss J.-A. Faull and Miss R. McQuillan
38 Miss L. Garrone and Miss K. Kschwendt
39 Miss S. L. Collins and Miss K. Radford
40 **Mrs. R. D. Fairbank-Nideffer and Miss B. Schultz** ⑮
41 **Miss J. Capriati and Miss M. Paz** ⑪
42 Miss J. Pospisilova and Miss E. Sviglerova
43 Miss L. Barnard and Miss A. B. Henricksson
44 Miss S. Appelmans and Miss C. M. Vis
45 Miss S. Graf and Miss C. Porwik
46 Miss H. Cioffi and Miss A. Frazier
(Q) 47 Miss J. Halard and Miss A. Huber
48 **Miss A. Sanchez Vicario and Miss H. Sukova** ③
49 **Miss N. Provis and Mrs. P. D. Smylie** ⑥
50 Mrs. R. Baranski and Miss T. J. Morton
51 Miss B. J. Cordwell and Miss C. Lindqvist
52 Miss I. Budarova and Miss A. Nohacova
53 Miss C. MacGregor and Mrs. H. L. Mager
(L) 54 Miss K. Date and Miss E. Iida
55 Miss L. Field and Miss M. Strandlund
56 **Miss K. M. Adams and Miss M. M. Bollegraf** ⑩
57 **Miss N. Tauziat and Mrs. H. Wiesner** ⑭
58 Miss K. Godridge and Miss G. Helgeson
59 Mrs. L. Gildemeister and Miss T. Scheuer-Larsen
60 Miss L. Spadea and Miss H. Ter Riet
61 Miss J. Limmer and Miss A. Woolcock
(L) 62 Miss M. Javer and Miss S. L. Smith
63 Miss C. Caverzasio and Miss N. Herreman
64 **Miss L. Savchenko and Miss N. Zvereva** ②

SECOND ROUND

Miss G. Fernandez and Miss J. Novotna ① 6-1, 6-1
Miss S. C. Rehe and Miss A. Temesvari 7-6 (7-1), 7-6 (7-3)
Miss B. Griffiths and Miss J. Wood 6-4, 6-4
Miss J. M. Hetherington and Miss K. S. Rinaldi ⑫ 6-3, 6-2
Miss S.C. Stafford and Miss T.S. Whitlinger 2-6, 6-2, 6-4
Miss B. A. Borneo and Miss C. J. Wood 6-3, 7-5
Miss E. S. Pfaff and Miss R. P. Stubbs 6-4, 4-6, 6-3
Mrs. S. W. Magers and Miss R. M. White ⑦ 7-5, 7-5
Miss M. J. Fernandez and Miss Z. L. Garrison ④ 6-2, 6-3
Miss G. E. Coorengel and Miss A. Van Buuren 6-4, 6-4
Miss M. Jaggard and Miss C. Suire 7-6 (7-0), 6-1
Miss C. Kohde-Kilsch and Miss E. Reinach ③ 6-3, 6-3
Miss L. J. Gregory and Miss A. May ⑯ 6-2, 4-6, 6-1
Miss R. Rajchrtova and Miss A. Strnadova 7-6 (8-10), 6-3, 7-5
Mrs. P. Paradis-Mangon and Miss A. Scott 7-5, 6-2
Miss K. Jordan and Miss L. M. McNeil ⑤ 6-2, 6-3
Miss M. Navratilova and Miss P. H. Shriver ⑧ 6-1, 6-0
Mrs. T. A. Harper and Miss M. Kidowaki 4-6, 7-6 (7-5), 6-4
Miss J.-A. Faull and Miss R. McQuillan 7-5, 4-6, 6-1
Mrs. R. D. Fairbank-Nideffer and Miss B. Schultz ⑮ 6-2, 1-6, 6-4
Miss J. Capriati and Miss M. Paz ⑪ 6-1, 6-4
Miss S. Appelmans and Miss C. M. Vis 6-4, 7-6 (7-4)
Miss H. Cioffi and Miss A. Frazier 7-6 (9-7), 1-6, 6-4
Miss A. Sanchez Vicario and Miss H. Sukova ③ 7-6 (7-4), 6-4
Miss N. Provis and Mrs. P. D. Smylie ⑥ 6-3, 6-1
Miss I. Budarova and Miss A. Nohacova 7-6 (7-3), 7-5
Miss K. Date and Miss E. Iida 6-4, 6-2
Miss K. M. Adams and Miss M. M. Bollegraf ⑩ 6-2, 7-6 (7-4)
Miss N. Tauziat and Mrs. H. Wiesner ④ 6-3, 7-5
Mrs. L. Gildemeister and Miss T. Scheuer-Larsen 6-4, 6-2
Miss M. Javer and Miss S. L. Smith 7-6 (7-4), 6-3
Miss L. Savchenko and Miss N. Zvereva ② 6-2, 6-2

THIRD ROUND

Miss G. Fernandez and Miss J. Novotna ① 6-7 (3-7), 6-4, 6-2
Miss J. M. Hetherington and Miss K. S. Rinaldi ⑫ 6-4, 6-2
Miss S. C. Stafford and Miss T. S. Whitlinger 6-2, 6-2
Mrs. S. W. Magers and Miss R. M. White ⑦ 6-2, 6-3
Miss M.J. Fernandez and Miss Z. L. Garrison ④ 6-1, 6-3
Miss C. Kohde-Kilsch and Miss E. Reinach ③ 6-4, 6-4
Miss R. Rajchrtova and Miss A. Strnadova 6-0, 7-5
Miss K. Jordan and Miss L. M. McNeil ⑤ 6-1, 6-1
Miss M. Navratilova and Miss P. H. Shriver ⑧ 6-4, 6-0
Miss J.-A. Faull and Miss R. McQuillan 6-2, 1-6, 6-4
Miss J. Capriati and Miss M. Paz ⑪ 6-2, 6-3
Miss A. Sanchez Vicario and Miss H. Sukova ③ 6-4, 6-1, 6-1
Miss N. Provis and Mrs. P. D. Smylie ⑥ 6-4, 6-2
Miss K. M. Adams and Miss M. M. Bollegraf ⑩ 7-6 (7-5), 6-3
Miss N. Tauziat and Mrs. H. Wiesner ④ 7-6 (10-8), 6-3
Miss L. Savchenko and Miss N. Zvereva ② 6-3, 6-3

QUARTER-FINALS

Miss G. Fernandez and Miss J. Novotna ① 6-2, 7-6 (7-4)
Mrs. S. W. Magers and Miss R. M. White ⑦ 6-2, 6-2
Miss M. J. Fernandez and Miss Z. L. Garrison ④ 6-3, 6-1
Miss K. Jordan and Miss L. M. McNeil ⑤ 6-2, 7-6 (7-3)
Miss M. Navratilova and Miss P. H. Shriver ⑧ 6-7 (5-7), 6-2, 6-2
Miss A. Sanchez Vicario and Miss H. Sukova ③ 6-2, 6-7 (7-9), 6-1
Miss K. M. Adams and Miss M. M. Bollegraf ⑩ 6-2, 7-6 (7-5)
Miss L. Savchenko and Miss N. Zvereva ② 6-1, 6-0

SEMI-FINALS

Miss G. Fernandez and Miss J. Novotna ① 6-3, 6-3
Miss M. J. Fernandez and Miss Z. L. Garrison ④ 4-6, 7-6 (7-3), 6-2
Miss M. Navratilova and Miss P. H. Shriver ⑧ 6-3, 7-6 (7-3)
Miss L. Savchenko and Miss N. Zvereva ② 2-6, 6-2, 6-4

FINAL

Miss G. Fernandez and Miss J. Novotna ① 7-5, 6-2
Miss L. Savchenko and Miss N. Zvereva ② 6-4, 3-6, 6-4

Winners: Miss L. Savchenko and Miss N. Zvereva ② 6-4, 3-6, 6-4

Heavy type denotes seeded players. The encircled figure against names denotes the order in which they have been seeded. (W) = Wild card. (Q) = Qualifier. (L) = Lucky loser. The Matches will be the best of three sets.

EVENT V.—THE MIXED DOUBLES CHAMPIONSHIP

Holders: R. LEACH and Miss Z. L. GARRISON

The Winners will become the holders, for the year, of the CHALLENGE CUP presented by the family of the late Mr. S. H. SMITH. The Winners will receive silver replicas of the Challenge Cup. A Silver Salver will be presented to each of the Runners-up and a Bronze Medal to each defeated Semi-finalist.

FIRST ROUND

1. **J. Pugh and Miss N. Zvereva** ①
2. N. Brown and Miss C. J. Wood
3. K. Evernden and Miss R. McQuillan
(Q) 4. S. Stolle and Miss N. Van Lottum
5. M. J. Bates and Miss J. M. Durie
6. N. Broad and Miss E. S. Pfaff
(L) 7. J. Morgan and Miss D. Jones
8. **J. Lozano and Miss A. Sanchez Vicario** ⑫
9. **W. Ferreira and Miss L. J. Gregory** ⑮
10. K. Kinnear and Miss C. Benjamin
11. C. Beckman and Mrs. T. A. Harper
12. H. Leconte and Miss S. Graf
13. P. Norval and Miss M. M. Bollegraf
(W) 14. M. R. J. Petchey and Miss S. J. Loosemore
(Q) 15. E. Amend and Miss H. A. Ludloff
16. **G. Michibata and Miss J. M. Hetherington** ⑥
17. **S. E. Davis and Miss R. M. White** ③
18. J. Canter and Miss A. May
19. M. Koevermans and Miss H. Ter Riet
20. D. MacPherson and Miss K. Godridge
21. B. Talbot and Miss B. J. Cordwell
22. S. Melville and Miss B. Somerville
23. B. Dyke and Miss M. Jaggard
24. **J. Grabb and Miss E. M. Burgin** ⑭
25. **T. A. Woodbridge and Miss N. Provis** ⑨
26. T. Nelson and Mrs. S. W. Magers
(W) 27. N. A. Fulwood and Miss S. L. Gomer
28. R. Smith and Miss C. Suire
(W) 29. R. Seguso and Mrs. C. K. Bassett-Seguso
30. U. Colombini and Miss L. Golarsa
31. K. Thorne and Miss S. Wibowo
32. **G. Connell and Miss K. S. Rinaldi** ⑧
33. **P. Galbraith and Miss P. A. Fendick** ⑤
(L) 34. M. Woodforde and Miss A. Frazier
35. J. Brown and Miss S. C. Stafford
(W) 36. C. J. Van Rensburg and Miss E. Reinach
37. N. Borwick and Miss A. Scott
38. J. Siemerink and Miss C. M. Vis
39. S. Youl and Miss L. Field
40. **M. Kratzmann and Miss P. H. Shriver** ⑯
41. **K. Flach and Miss K. Jordan** ⑪
42. S. Cannon and Miss K. M. Adams
43. R. W. Van't Hof and Miss C. MacGregor
44. S. Salumaa and Miss K. Kschwendt
45. M. Schapers and Miss B. Schultz
46. T. Nijssen and Miss A. Temesvari
47. S. Kruger and Miss A. Strnadova
48. **R. Leach and Miss Z. L. Garrison** ④
(L) 49. L. J. Bale and Miss A. Van Buuren
50. S. Devries and Miss N. Miyagi
51. J. Rive and Miss S. L. Collins
52. L. Warder and Miss J.-A. Faull
53. J. Stoltenberg and Miss R. P. Stubbs
(W) 54. T. S. Mayotte and Miss G. Fernandez
(Q) 55. A. Kratzmann and Miss K.-A. Guse
56. **D. T. Visser and Mrs. R. D. Fairbank-Nideffer** ⑩
57. **C. Suk and Miss H. Sukova** ③
58. B. Shelton and Miss L. M. McNeil
59. B. Garnett and Miss C. Bakkum
60. T. Svantesson and Miss T. S. Whitlinger
61. L. Pimek and Miss L. Savchenko
62. G. Van Emburgh and Mrs. H. L. Mager
63. P. Annacone and Miss S. C. Rehe
64. **J. B. Fitzgerald and Mrs. P. D. Smylie** ②

SECOND ROUND

- J. Pugh and Miss N. Zvereva ① — 6-2, 6-3
- K. Evernden and Miss R. McQuillan — 3-6, 6-3, 6-4
- M. J. Bates and Miss J. M. Durie — 6-3, 6-2
- J. Lozano and Miss A. Sanchez Vicario ⑫ — 7-5, 6-3
- K. Kinnear and Miss C. Benjamin — 2-6, 6-4, 14-12
- H. Leconte and Miss S. Graf — 6-1, 6-2
- P. Norval and Miss M. M. Bollegraf — 4-6, 6-4, 6-1
- G. Michibata and Miss J. M. Hetherington ⑥ — 6-4, 6-7 (2-7), 9-7
- J. Canter and Miss A. May — 6-3, 6-4
- M. Koevermans and Miss H. Ter Riet — 4-6, 6-3, 6-4
- B. Talbot and Miss B. J. Cordwell — 7-6 (7-3), 6-7 (7-9), 6-1
- B. Dyke and Miss M. Jaggard — 6-3, 6-3
- T. A. Woodbridge and Miss N. Provis ⑨ — 6-2, 6-2
- R. Smith and Miss C. Suire — 7-5, 7-5
- U. Colombini and Miss L. Golarsa — 6-2, 4-6, 9-7
- G. Connell and Miss K. S. Rinaldi ⑧ — 6-4, 6-3
- M. Woodforde and Miss A. Frazier — 6-1, 1-6, 6-4
- C. J. Van Rensburg and Miss E. Reinach — 6-2, 2-6, 6-3
- J. Siemerink and Miss C. M. Vis — 4-6, 6-3, 12-10
- M. Kratzmann and Miss P. H. Shriver ⑯ — 6-1, 6-2
- K. Flach and Miss K. Jordan ⑪ — 7-6 (7-5), 6-4
- S. Salumaa and Miss K. Kschwendt — 4-6, 6-1, 11-9
- M. Schapers and Miss B. Schultz — 6-3, 5-7, 29-27
- R. Leach and Miss Z. L. Garrison ④ — 3-6, 6-1, 6-2
- S. Devries and Miss N. Miyagi — 6-3, 7-6 (7-3)
- J. Rive and Miss S. L. Collins — 6-7 (3-7), 6-4, 6-2
- J. Stoltenberg and Miss R. P. Stubbs — 4-6, 6-2, 6-2
- D. T. Visser and Mrs. R. D. Fairbank-Nideffer ⑩ — 6-4, 6-2
- C. Suk and Miss H. Sukova ③ — 7-6 (8-6), 6-7 (6-8), 6-2
- B. Garnett and Miss C. Bakkum — 6-4, 6-2
- L. Pimek and Miss L. Savchenko — 4-6, 6-4, 6-3
- J. B. Fitzgerald and Mrs. P. D. Smylie ② — 6-4, 6-3

THIRD ROUND

- J. Pugh and Miss N. Zvereva ① — 2-6, 6-3, 6-4
- M. J. Bates and Miss J. M. Durie — 6-4, 6-4
- H. Leconte and Miss S. Graf — 6-2, 7-5
- G. Michibata and Miss J. M. Hetherington ⑥ — 7-6 (7-5), 7-6 (7-4)
- M. Koevermans and Miss H. Ter Riet — 7-5, 6-7 (7-9), 6-4
- B. Dyke and Miss M. Jaggard — 6-4, 6-7 (6-8), 6-3
- T. A. Woodbridge and Miss N. Provis ⑨ — 7-5, 6-3
- G. Connell and Miss K. S. Rinaldi ⑧ — 5-7, 6-1, 6-4
- C. J. Van Rensburg and Miss E. Reinach — 6-4, 6-1
- J. Siemerink and Miss C. M. Vis — 7-6 (7-5), 3-6, 10-8
- S. Salumaa and Miss K. Kschwendt — 6-4, 6-3
- M. Schapers and Miss B. Schultz — 3-6, 6-3, 13-11
- S. Devries and Miss N. Miyagi — 4-6, 6-3, 6-4
- J. Stoltenberg and Miss R. P. Stubbs — 3-6, 6-3, 6-2
- C. Suk and Miss H. Sukova ③ — 7-6 (7-5), 7-6 (7-4)
- J. B. Fitzgerald and Mrs. P. D. Smylie ② — 6-3, 6-2

QUARTER-FINALS

- J. Pugh and Miss N. Zvereva ① — 7-5, 6-4
- G. Michibata and Miss J. M. Hetherington ⑥ — 6-4, 7-6 (7-4)
- B. Dyke and Miss M. Jaggard — 6-2, 6-3
- G. Connell and Miss K. S. Rinaldi ⑧ — 5-7, 7-6 (7-3), 6-4
- C. J. Van Rensburg and Miss E. Reinach — 6-2, 6-2
- M. Schapers and Miss B. Schultz — 3-6, 6-2, 6-1
- J. Stoltenberg and Miss R. P. Stubbs — 7-6 (7-5), 6-3
- J. B. Fitzgerald and Mrs. P. D. Smylie ② — 6-3, 6-4

SEMI-FINALS

- J. Pugh and Miss N. Zvereva ① — 6-4, 6-3
- G. Connell and Miss K. S. Rinaldi ⑧ — 6-4, 6-4
- C. J. Van Rensburg and Miss E. Reinach — 7-6 (7-5), 7-6 (7-5)
- J. B. Fitzgerald and Mrs. P. D. Smylie ② — 6-4, 6-2

FINAL

- J. Pugh and Miss N. Zvereva ① — 7-5, 6-2
- J. B. Fitzgerald and Mrs. P. D. Smylie ② — 7-5, 3-6, 7-5

WINNER

J. B. Fitzgerald and Mrs. P. D. Smylie ② — 7-6 (7-4), 6-2

Heavy type denotes seeded players. The encircled figure against names denotes the order in which they have been seeded. (W) = Wild card. (Q) = Qualifier. (L) = Lucky loser. The Matches will be the best of three sets.

149

EVENT VI.—THE 35 AND OVER GENTLEMEN'S INVITATION SINGLES

Holder: T. R. GULLIKSON

The Winner will become the holder, for the year only, of a Cup presented by The All England Lawn Tennis and Croquet Club. The Winner will receive a miniature Silver Salver, the Runner-up will be presented with a Silver Medal.

	FIRST ROUND		QUARTER-FINALS	SEMI-FINALS	FINAL
1	**T. R. Gullikson** ①	(USA)	**T. R. Gullikson** ①	**T. R. Gullikson** ① 4–6, 6–3, 6–2	
2	Bye				
3	V. Amritraj	(IND)	J. G. Alexander 6–2, 7–6 (7–2)		
4	J. G. Alexander	(AUS)			
5	**J. M. Lloyd** ③	(GBR)	**J. M. Lloyd** ③	**J. M. Lloyd** ③ 6–4, 7–6 (7–4)	
6	Bye				
7	S. R. Smith	(USA)	S. R. Smith 6–4, 6–3		
8	P. F. McNamee	(AUS)			
9	A. A. Mayer	(USA)	A. A. Mayer 6–3, 3–6, 6–1	**P. Fleming** ④ 6–4, Retd.	
10	P. C. Dent	(AUS)			
11	Bye		**P. Fleming** ④		
12	**P. Fleming** ④	(USA)			
13	T. S. Okker	(HOL)	R. L. Stockton 6–3, 6–3	**T. E. Gullikson** ② 6–4, 4–6, 6–3	
14	R. L. Stockton	(USA)			
15	Bye		**T. E. Gullikson** ②		
16	**T. E. Gullikson** ②	(USA)			

J. M. Lloyd ③ 7–6 (7–4), 3–6, 7–5 · **T. E. Gullikson** ② 6–4, 6–2 · **T. E. Gullikson** ② 7–6 (9–7), 3–6, 6–2

Heavy type denotes seeded players. The encircled figure against names denotes the order in which they have been seeded. The Matches will be the best of three sets.
The tie-break will operate at six games all in all three sets.

Event VII.—THE 35 AND OVER GENTLEMEN'S INVITATION DOUBLES   Holders: P. McNAMARA and P. F. McNAMEE

The Winners will become the holders, for the year only, of a Cup presented by The All England Lawn Tennis and Croquet Club. The Winners will receive miniature Silver Salvers, a Silver Medal will be presented to each of the Runners-up.

FIRST ROUND	QUARTER-FINALS	SEMI-FINALS	FINAL
1 P. McNamara and P. F. McNamee ①	P. McNamara and P. F. McNamee ① 6–3, 6–3	P. McNamara and P. F. McNamee ① 6–3, 6–4	
2 J. Kodes and A. Metreveli			
3 N. Pilic and B. Taroczy	N. Pilic and B. Taroczy 6–3, 6–4		
4 J. D. Newcombe and A. D. Roche			
5 P. Slozil and T. Smid ③	P. Slozil and T. Smid ③ 6–4, 6–4	P. Slozil and T. Smid ③ 6–2, 6–3	
6 J. G. Alexander and P. C. Dent			
7 M. C. Riessen and S. E. Stewart	K. R. Rosewall and F. S. Stolle 7–6 (7–3), 4–6, 6–3		
8 K. R. Rosewall and F. S. Stolle			
9 I. Nastase and R. Taylor	R. A. J. Hewitt and F. D. McMillan 7–5, 6–2	R. L. Stockton and E. J. Van Dillen 6–3, 6–4	
10 R. A. J. Hewitt and F. D. McMillan			
11 R. L. Stockton and E. J. Van Dillen	R. L. Stockton and E. J. Van Dillen 7–5, 6–3		
12 A. Amritraj and V. Amritraj ④			
13 P. Fleming and S. R. Smith	P. Fleming and S. R. Smith 6–0, 6–3	P. Fleming and S. R. Smith 6–4, 7–6 (7–4)	
14 R. L. Case and G. Masters			
15 C. Dowdeswell and A. J. Stone	C. Dowdeswell and A. J. Stone 6–4, 2–6, 9–7		
16 T. E. Gullikson and T. R. Gullikson ②			

FINAL column:
P. McNamara and P. F. McNamee ① 5–7, 7–5, 6–1
P. Fleming and S. R. Smith 7–5, 6–7 (5–7), 6–4

Winner: P. Fleming and S. R. Smith 7–6 (7–4), 7–6 (7–4)

Heavy type denotes seeded players. The encircled figure against names denotes the order in which they have been seeded. The Matches will be the best of three sets.
The tie-break will operate at six games all in the first two sets.

Event VIII.—THE 35 AND OVER LADIES' INVITATION DOUBLES   Holders: Miss W.M. TURNBULL and Miss S.V. WADE

The Winners will become the holders, for the year only, of a Cup presented by The All England Lawn Tennis and Croquet Club. The Winners will receive miniature Cups, a Silver Medal will be presented to each of the Runners-up.

FIRST ROUND	SEMI-FINALS	FINAL
1 Miss W. M. Turnbull and Miss S. V. Wade ①	Miss W. M. Turnbull and Miss S. V. Wade ① 6–2, 6–0	Miss W. M. Turnbull and Miss S. V. Wade ① 6–2, 6–2
2 Miss M. E. A. Bueno and Miss O. Morozova		
3 Mrs. R. Cawley and Mrs. G. E. Reid ③	Mrs. F. Durr and Miss B. F. Stove 3–6, 6–4, 6–2	
4 Mrs. F. Durr and Miss B. F. Stove		
5 Miss M. Michel and Miss V. J. Ziegenfuss	Mrs. D. E. Dalton and Miss J. C. Russell ④ 6–4, 6–2	Miss R. Casals and Mrs. M. H. Pete ② 6–4, 6–3
6 Mrs. D. E. Dalton and Miss J. C. Russell ④		
7 Miss S. Barker and Miss L. J. Charles	Miss R. Casals and Mrs. M. H. Pete ② 6–2, 6–3	
8 Miss R. Casals and Mrs. M. H. Pete ②		

FINAL column:
Miss W. M. Turnbull and Miss S. V. Wade ① 6–3, 6–4

Winner: Miss W. M. Turnbull and Miss S. V. Wade ①

Heavy type denotes seeded players. The encircled figure against names denotes the order in which they have been seeded. The Matches will be the best of three sets.
The tie-break will operate at six games all in the first two sets.

EVENT IX.—THE BOYS' SINGLES CHAMPIONSHIP

Holder: L. PAES

The Winner will become the holder, for the year only, of a Cup presented by The All England Lawn Tennis and Croquet Club. The Winner and Runner-up will each receive a personal prize.

FIRST ROUND

1. **K. Alami** ① (MAR)
2. P. Delgado (CHI)
3. E. Casas (MEX)
4. M. Joyce (USA)
5. H. Kaneko (JPN)
6. P. C. Robinson (GBR)
7. J. S. Greenhalgh (NZL)
8. **H.-K. Song** ⑯ (KOR)
9. **J. Eagle** ⑩ (AUS)
10. R. Reddy (IND)
11. J.-L. De Jager (RSA)
12. S. Sargsian (URS)
13. A. Larsen (DEN)
14. J. Holmes (AUS)
15. M. Martinelle (SWE)
16. **B. Wijaya** ⑧ (INA)
17. **D. Witt** ④ (USA)
18. J. Unterberger (AUT)
19. E. Udozorh (NGR)
20. J. N. R. Baily (GBR)
21. D. Prchlik (TCH)
22. N. Kirtane (IND)
23. R. Sujevic (YUG)
24. **S. Gessner** ⑬ (GER)
25. **G. Rusedski** ⑫ (CAN)
26. F. Ruiz (CHI)
27. C. B. Wheeler (GBR)
28. F. Setiawan (INA)
29. B. Dunn (USA)
30. A. Urencio (MEX)
31. S. Yongchantanasakul (THA)
32. **G. Doyle** ⑥ (AUS)
33. **D. Prinosil** ⑤ (GER)
34. J. Knowle (AUT)
35. M. Navarro (ITA)
36. L. Arnold (ARG)
37. C. M. MacLagan (GBR)
38. V. Jovanovic (YUG)
39. G. Steenkamp (RSA)
40. **P. Kilderry** ⑪ (AUS)
41. **K. Carlsen** ⑭ (DEN)
42. S. Ladipo (NGR)
43. S. Kirtane (IND)
44. J. Leach (USA)
45. C. Tarantino (ARG)
46. M. Schofield (GBR)
47. D. Waworuntu (INA)
48. **A. Medvedev** ③ (URS)
49. **J. I. Garat** ⑦ (ARG)
50. G. Zgola (POL)
51. A. Radulescu (GER)
52. E. Abaroa (MEX)
53. G. Silberstein (CHI)
54. N. Godwin (RSA)
55. V. Spadea (USA)
56. **P. Gazda** ⑨ (TCH)
57. **S. Gleeson** ⑮ (AUS)
58. T. Chaen (JPN)
59. M. Bhupathi (IND)
60. L. J. Sabin (GBR)
61. N. Ploysook (THA)
62. N. Kischkewitz (FRA)
63. J. Elola (URU)
64. **T. Enqvist** ② (SWE)

SECOND ROUND

- K. Alami ① — 6-4, 6-1
- M. Joyce — 6-3, 6-3
- H. Kaneko — 6-3, 6-3
- H.-K. Song ⑯ — 6-1, 6-3
- J. Eagle ⑩ — 6-3, 6-1
- S. Sargsian — 6-2, 4-6, 10-8
- J. Holmes — 6-1, 6-1
- B. Wijaya ⑧ — 6-3, 7-6 (7-3)
- J. Unterberger — 7-6 (7-2), 4-6, 6-3
- J. N. R. Baily — 6-1, 6-4
- D. Prchlik — 6-3, 7-5
- S. Gessner ⑬ — 6-2, 6-3
- G. Rusedski ⑫ — 6-3, 6-3
- F. Setiawan — 7-5, 7-6 (8-6)
- B. Dunn — 6-1, 6-4
- G. Doyle ⑥ — 6-1, 6-2
- D. Prinosil ⑤ — 6-1, 6-2
- M. Navarro — 6-1, 7-6 (7-5)
- C. M. MacLagan — 6-2, 6-7 (3-7), 6-0
- P. Kilderry ⑪ — 6-4, 6-2
- K. Carlsen ⑭ — 6-4, 5-7, 6-3
- J. Leach — 7-6 (7-2), 7-5
- M. Schofield — 6-3, 6-4
- A. Medvedev ③ — 6-4, 6-3
- J. I. Garat ⑦ — 6-1, 6-3
- A. Radulescu — 6-4, 7-5
- N. Godwin — 6-2, 6-4
- V. Spadea — 7-5, 6-4
- S. Gleeson ⑮ — 7-6 (12-10), 7-6 (7-0)
- M. Bhupathi — 7-5, 6-3
- N. Kischkewitz — 6-3, 6-3
- T. Enqvist ② — 7-6 (7-2), 6-3

THIRD ROUND

- M. Joyce — 3-6, 7-5, 6-3
- H.-K. Song ⑯ — 6-2, 7-5
- S. Sargsian — 7-6 (7-1), 6-2
- J. Holmes — 7-6 (7-2), 6-7 (2-7), 6-4
- J. Unterberger — 6-4, 7-5
- S. Gessner ⑬ — 6-1, 6-3
- G. Rusedski ⑫ — 6-2, 6-2
- G. Doyle ⑥ — 6-4, 6-3
- M. Navarro — 6-4, 6-4
- P. Kilderry ⑪ — 6-3, 5-7, 6-0
- K. Carlsen ⑭ — 6-3, 4-6, 6-4
- A. Medvedev ③ — 6-4, 6-2
- A. Radulescu — 2-6, 6-2, 6-4
- V. Spadea — 7-6 (7-5), 6-2
- S. Gleeson ⑮ — 6-2, 6-2
- T. Enqvist ② — 6-4, 7-5

QUARTER-FINALS

- M. Joyce — 6-2, 6-4
- J. Holmes — 6-7 (4-7), 6-4, 6-2
- S. Gessner ⑬ — 6-4, 6-7 (2-7), 6-3
- G. Rusedski ⑫ — 6-4, 6-2
- P. Kilderry ⑪ — 6-3, 6-4
- K. Carlsen ⑭ — 6-1, 6-3
- V. Spadea — 7-5, 6-4
- T. Enqvist ② — 7-6 (7-5), 6-1

SEMI-FINALS

- M. Joyce — 6-4, 3-6, 6-3
- G. Rusedski ⑫ — 7-5, 6-2
- P. Kilderry ⑪ — 7-6 (7-4), 7-6 (7-5)
- T. Enqvist ② — 6-7 (2-7), 6-4, 6-3

FINAL

- M. Joyce — 6-2, 6-4
- T. Enqvist ② — 6-2, 6-2

Champion: T. Enqvist ② — 6-4, 6-3

Heavy type denotes seeded players. The encircled figure against names denotes the order in which they have been seeded. The Committee reserves the right to alter the seeding order in the event of withdrawals. The Matches will be the best of three sets.

EVENT X.—THE BOYS' DOUBLES CHAMPIONSHIP

Holders: S. LAREAU and S. LEBLANC

The Winners will become the holders, for the year only, of a Cup presented by The All England Lawn Tennis and Croquet Club. The Winners and Runners-up will each receive a personal prize.

FIRST ROUND

1. **G. Doyle and J. Eagle** ①
2. P. Gazda and D. Prchlik
3. K. Carlsen and A. Larsen
4. J. I. Garat and T. Winkler
5. **J.-L. De Jager and A. Medvedev** ③
6. S. Gleeson and P. C. Robinson
7. J. Leach and D. Witt
8. S. Ladipo and E. Udozorh
9. M. Joyce and V. Spadea
10. C. M. MacLagan and M. Schofield
11. H.-K. Song and B. Wijaya
12. **K. Alami and G. Rusedski** ④
13. J. Knowle and J. Unterberger
14. T. Enqvist and M. Martinelle
15. E. Abaroa and E. Casas
16. **J. Holmes and P. Kilderry** ②

QUARTER-FINALS

- G. Doyle and J. Eagle ① — 6-2, 6-4
- K. Carlsen and A. Larsen — 6-4, 6-4
- J.-L. De Jager and A. Medvedev ③ — 3-6, 6-1, 6-4
- J. Leach and D. Witt — 6-2, 6-2
- M. Joyce and V. Spadea — 6-3, 6-2
- K. Alami and G. Rusedski ④ — 6-3, 6-4
- T. Enqvist and M. Martinelle — 6-3, 7-5
- J. Holmes and P. Kilderry ② — 6-7 (7-9), 6-3, 6-3

SEMI-FINALS

- K. Carlsen and A. Larsen — 6-4, 3-6, 7-5
- J.-L. De Jager and A. Medvedev ③ — 6-1, 6-4
- K. Alami and G. Rusedski ④ — 7-6 (10-8), 3-6, 12-10
- J. Holmes and P. Kilderry ② — 6-3, 6-2

FINAL

- J.-L. De Jager and A. Medvedev ③ — 6-3, 6-2
- K. Alami and G. Rusedski ④ — 6-3, 4-6, 6-4

Champions: K. Alami and G. Rusedski ④ — 1-6, 7-6 (7-4), 6-4

Heavy type denotes seeded players. The encircled figure against names denotes the order in which they have been seeded. The Committee reserves the right to alter the seeding order in the event of withdrawals. The Matches will be the best of three sets.

EVENT XI.—THE GIRLS' SINGLES CHAMPIONSHIP

Holder: Miss A. STRNADOVA

The Winner will become the holder, for the year only, of a Cup presented by The All England Lawn Tennis and Croquet Club. The Winner and Runner-up will each receive a personal prize.

	FIRST ROUND		SECOND ROUND		THIRD ROUND		QUARTER-FINALS		SEMI-FINALS	FINAL
1	**Miss B. Rittner** ①	(GER)	**Miss B. Rittner** ①	6-4, 6-1	Miss B. Rittner ①	6-4, 6-1	Miss B. Rittner ①	2-6, 6-1, 6-1	Miss B. Rittner ① 7-6 (7-4), 6-1	Miss B. Rittner ① 3-6, 6-1, 6-2
2	Miss M. Muric	(YUG)								
3	Miss L. Niemantsverdriet	(HOL)	Miss L. Niemantsverdriet	6-3, 6-4						
4	Miss A. Woolcock	(AUS)					Miss M. J. Gaidano ⑮ 4-6, 7-5, 6-2			
5	Miss D. Merchant	(AUT)	Miss K. Buche	6-2, 6-2	Miss M. J. Gaidano ⑮ 6-1, 6-1					
6	Miss K. Buche	(GER)								
7	Miss M. A. Quezada	(CHI)	**Miss M. J. Gaidano** ⑮	6-1, 6-1						
8	**Miss M. J. Gaidano** ⑮	(ARG)								
9	**Miss C. Barclay** ⑨	(AUS)	Miss J. M. Pullin	6-4, 7-5						
10	Miss J. M. Pullin	(GBR)			Miss R. De Los Rios 6-2, 6-4					
11	Miss H. Matthews	(GBR)	Miss R. De Los Rios	6-3, 6-2			Miss R. De Los Rios 6-4, 4-6, 6-4			
12	Miss R. De Los Rios	(PAR)								
13	Miss K. Cross	(GBR)	Miss J. Feria	6-3, 4-6, 6-4	Miss J. Limmer ⑧ 6-1, 6-4					
14	Miss J. Feria	(PHI)								
15	Miss C. Summers	(RSA)	**Miss J. Limmer** ⑧	6-1, 7-5						
16	**Miss J. Limmer** ⑧	(AUS)								
17	**Miss N. Pratt** ④	(AUS)	**Miss N. Pratt** ④	6-0, 6-2	Miss N. Pratt ④ 7-5, 6-3			Miss P. Nelson ⑥ 6-3, 6-4		
18	Miss S. Duangchan	(THA)					Miss S.-H. Park ⑬ 6-3, 7-6 (7-3)			
19	Miss E. Martincova	(TCH)	Miss E. Martincova	6-3, 6-0						
20	Miss I. Majoli	(YUG)								
21	Miss C. M. Hunt	(GBR)	Miss L. Zaltz	6-4, 6-2	Miss S.-H. Park ⑬ 6-2, 6-4					
22	Miss L. Zaltz	(ISR)								
23	Miss A. C. Vaughan	(ZIM)	**Miss S.-H. Park** ⑬	6-0, 6-1						
24	**Miss S.-H. Park** ⑬	(KOR)								
25	**Miss A. I. Sugiyama** ⑪	(JPN)	**Miss A. I. Sugiyama** ⑪	6-4, 6-4	Miss A. I. Sugiyama ⑪ 6-3, 6-0		Miss P. Nelson ⑥ 1-6, 6-4, 6-3			
26	Miss L. Schaerer	(PAR)								
27	Miss P. Soerensen	(DEN)	Miss S.-A. Siddall	6-3, 6-3						
28	Miss S.-A. Siddall	(GBR)								
29	Miss J. Schad	(DOM)	Miss J. Schad	6-0, 6-4	Miss P. Nelson ⑥ 6-2, 6-2					
30	Miss W. H. Nguyen	(GUM)								
31	Miss M. Chernovita	(INA)	**Miss P. Nelson** ⑥	6-3, 6-1						
32	**Miss P. Nelson** ⑥	(USA)								
33	**Miss C. Rubin** ⑤	(USA)	**Miss C. Rubin** ⑤	6-4, 6-2	Miss C. Rubin ⑤ 2-6, 6-4, 6-3		Miss C. Rubin ⑤ 6-0, 6-4		Miss E. Makarova 6-4, 3-6, 6-3	Miss B. Rittner ① 6-7 (6-8), 6-2, 6-3
34	Miss W. Martinez	(MEX)								
35	Miss M. Donoshiro	(JPN)	Miss M. Donoshiro	6-3, 6-4						
36	Miss G. Devercelle	(PER)								
37	Miss E. Gevers	(RSA)	Miss E. Gevers	6-1, 0-6, 6-2	Miss A. Smashnova ⑫ 6-1, 6-3					
38	Miss F. M. La'o	(PHI)								
39	Miss K. Takuma	(JPN)	**Miss A. Smashnova** ⑫	6-3, 6-1						
40	**Miss A. Smashnova** ⑫	(ISR)								
41	**Miss J. Kruger** ⑭	(RSA)	**Miss J. Kruger** ④	6-2, 6-2	Miss E. Makarova 6-3, 6-4		Miss E. Makarova 6-1, 6-2			
42	Miss C. Instebo	(NOR)								
43	Miss E. Makarova	(URS)	Miss E. Makarova	6-2, 6-2						
44	Miss M. F. Cianfagna	(ARG)								
45	Miss V. Valdovinos	(PAR)	Miss A. M. H. Wainwright	6-2, 6-3	Miss A. M. H. Wainwright 2-6, 6-2, 7-5					
46	**Miss A. M. H. Wainwright**	(GBR)								
47	Miss A. Reddy	(IND)	Miss A. Reddy	6-4, 6-3						
48	Miss J. Ward	(GBR)								
49	**Miss S. L. Bentley** ⑦	(GBR)	Miss Y. Tanaka	4-6, 6-4, 6-3	Miss Y. Tanaka 6-4, 2-6, 6-4			Miss Z. Malkova ⑩ 7-5, 6-1		
50	Miss Y. Tanaka	(JPN)								
51	Miss B. Jankovic	(YUG)	Miss B. Sangaram	6-3, 2-6, 6-3						
52	Miss B. Sangaram	(THA)								
53	Miss N. Simunic	(RSA)	Miss N. Simunic	6-2, 6-1	Miss Z. Malkova ⑩ 4-1, Retd.					
54	Miss J. J. Saret	(PHI)								
55	Miss J. Foillard	(FRA)	**Miss Z. Malkova** ⑩	6-3, 6-2						
56	**Miss Z. Malkova** ⑩	(TCH)								
57	**Miss M. Babel** ⑯	(GER)	Miss K. Boogert	6-2, 7-6 (7-3)	Miss K. Boogert 6-2, 6-7 (5-7), 10-8		Miss K. Godridge ② 6-3, 4-6, 6-2		Miss K. Godridge ② 6-4, 6-4	
58	Miss K. Boogert	(HOL)								
59	Miss C. Hall	(GBR)	Miss C. Hall	4-6, 7-5, 6-1						
60	Miss N. Hummel	(USA)								
61	Miss R. Grande	(ITA)	Miss R. Grande	6-0, 6-1	Miss K. Godridge ② 6-2, 3-6, 8-6					
62	Miss C. Ampuero	(BOL)								
63	Miss L. Olave	(URU)	**Miss K. Godridge** ②	6-1, 6-1						
64	**Miss K. Godridge** ②	(AUS)								

Heavy type denotes seeded players. The encircled figure against names denotes the order in which they have been seeded. The Committee reserves the right to alter the seeding order in the event of withdrawals. The Matches will be the best of three sets.

EVENT XII.—THE GIRLS' DOUBLES CHAMPIONSHIP

Holders: Miss K. HABSUDOVA and Miss A. STRNADOVA

The Winners will become the holders, for the year only, of a Cup presented by The All England Lawn Tennis and Croquet Club. The Winners and Runners-up will each receive a personal prize.

	FIRST ROUND	QUARTER-FINALS		SEMI-FINALS	FINAL
1	Miss K. Godridge and Miss N. Pratt ①	Miss S. Duangchan and Miss B. Sangaram	6-2, 6-0	Miss S.-H. Park and Miss J. J. Saret 2-6, 7-6 (7-3), 6-3	Miss C. Barclay and Miss L. Zaltz ④ 5-7, 6-4, 6-4
2	Miss S. Duangchan and Miss B. Sangaram				
3	Miss S. L. Bentley and Miss C. M. Hunt	Miss S.-H. Park and Miss J. J. Saret	7-5, 6-3		
4	Miss S.-H. Park and Miss J. J. Saret				
5	**Miss C. Barclay and Miss L. Zaltz** ④	**Miss C. Barclay and Miss L. Zaltz** ④	6-1, 5-7, 6-3	Miss C. Barclay and Miss L. Zaltz ④ 6-3, 6-2	
6	Miss K. Boogert and Miss L. Niemantsverdriet				
7	Miss C. Hall and Miss S.-A. Siddall	Miss J. Kruger and Miss C. Summers	6-3, 3-6, 6-1		
8	Miss J. Kruger and Miss C. Summers				
9	Miss E. Makarova and Miss M. Muric	Miss E. Makarova and Miss M. Muric	4-6, 6-4, 8-6	Miss E. Makarova and Miss M. Muric 6-4, 6-4	Miss J. Limmer and Miss A. Woolcock ② 3-6, 6-3, 6-3
10	Miss M. Babel and Miss B. Rittner				
11	Miss R. De Los Rios and Miss L. Schaerer	**Miss Z. Malkova and Miss E. Martincova** ③	6-4, 3-6, 6-0		
12	**Miss Z. Malkova and Miss E. Martincova** ③				
13	Miss J. M. Pullin and Miss A. M. H. Wainwright	Miss P. Nelson and Miss C. Rubin	6-2, 6-3	Miss J. Limmer and Miss A. Woolcock ② 5-7, 6-1, 8-6	
14	Miss P. Nelson and Miss C. Rubin				
15	Miss M. Donoshiro and Miss A. I. Sugiyama	**Miss J. Limmer and Miss A. Woolcock** ②	3-6, 6-4, 6-4		
16	**Miss J. Limmer and Miss A. Woolcock** ②				

Final: Miss C. Barclay and Miss L. Zaltz ④ 6-4, 6-4

Heavy type denotes seeded players. The encircled figure against names denotes the order in which they have been seeded. The Committee reserves the right to alter the seeding order in the event of withdrawals. The Matches will be the best of three sets.

COUNTRIES IN THIS YEARS CHAMPIONSHIPS
ABBREVIATIONS

ARG	Argentina	DEN	Denmark	ISR	Israel	PAR	Paraguay	THA	Thailand
AUS	Australia	DOM	Dominican Republic	ITA	Italy	PER	Peru	USA	United States
AUT	Austria	FIN	Finland	JPN	Japan	PHI	Philippines	URS	Union of Soviet Social Republics
BAH	Bahamas	FRA	France	KOR	Korea	POL	Poland	URU	Uruguay
BEL	Belgium	GER	Germany	LUX	Luxembourg	POR	Portugal	VEN	Venezuela
BOL	Bolivia	GBR	Great Britain	MAR	Morocco	PUR	Puerto Rico	YUG	Yugoslavia
BRA	Brazil	GUM	Guam	MEX	Mexico	ROM	Romania	ZIM	Zimbabwe
BUL	Bulgaria	HUN	Hungary	HOL	Netherlands	RSA	South Africa		
CAN	Canada	IND	India	NZL	New Zealand	ESP	Spain		
CHI	Chile	INA	Indonesia	NIG	Nigeria	SWE	Sweden		
TCH	Czechoslovakia	IRN	Iran	NOR	Norway	SUI	Switzerland		

THE CHAMPIONSHIP ROLL
Champions and Runners-up

MEN'S SINGLES

1877—S. W. Gore
W. C. Marshall
1878—P. F. Hadow
S. W. Gore
★1879—J. T. Hartley
V. St L. Goold
1880—J. T. Hartley
H. F. Lawford
1881—W. Renshaw
J. T. Hartley
1882—W. Renshaw
E. Renshaw
1883—W. Renshaw
E. Renshaw
1884—W. Renshaw
H. F. Lawford
1885—W. Renshaw
H. F. Lawford
1886—W. Renshaw
H. F. Lawford
★1887—H. F. Lawford
E. Renshaw
1888—E. Renshaw
H. F. Lawford
1889—W. Renshaw
E. Renshaw
1890—W. J. Hamilton
W. Renshaw
★1891—W. Baddeley
J. Pim
1892—W. Baddeley
J. Pim
1893—J. Pim
W. Baddeley
1894—J. Pim
W. Baddeley
★1895—W. Baddeley
W. V. Eaves

1896—H. S. Mahony
W. Baddeley
1897—R. F. Doherty
H. S. Mahony
1898—R. F. Doherty
H. L. Doherty
1899—R. F. Doherty
A. W. Gore
1900—R. F. Doherty
S. H. Smith
1901—A. W. Gore
R. F. Doherty
1902—H. L. Doherty
A. W. Gore
1903—H. L. Doherty
F. L. Riseley
1904—H. L. Doherty
F. L. Riseley
1905—H. L. Doherty
N. E. Brookes
1906—H. L. Doherty
F. L. Riseley
★1907—N. E. Brookes
A. W. Gore
★1908—A. W. Gore
H. Roper Barrett
1909—A. W. Gore
M. J. G. Ritchie
1910—A. F. Wilding
A. W. Gore
1911—A. F. Wilding
H. Roper Barrett
1912—A. F. Wilding
A. W. Gore
1913—A. F. Wilding
M. E. McLoughlin
1914—N. E. Brookes
A. F. Wilding

1919—G. L. Patterson
N. E. Brookes
1920—W. T. Tilden
G. L. Patterson
1921—W. T. Tilden
B. I. C. Norton
★†1922—G. L. Patterson
R. Lycett
1923—W. M. Johnston
F. T. Hunter
1924—J. Borotra
R. Lacoste
1925—R. Lacoste
J. Borotra
1926—J. Borotra
H. Kinsey
1927—H. Cochet
J. Borotra
1928—R. Lacoste
H. Cochet
1929—H. Cochet
J. Borotra
1930—W. T. Tilden
W. Allison
1931—S. B. Wood
F. X. Shields
1932—H. E. Vines
H. W. Austin
1933—J. H. Crawford
H. E. Vines
1934—F. J. Perry
J. H. Crawford
1935—F. J. Perry
G. von Cramm
1936—F. J. Perry
G. von Cramm
★1937—J. D. Budge
G. von Cramm

1938—J. D. Budge
H. W. Austin
★1939—R. L. Riggs
E. T. Cooke
★1946—Y. Petra
G. E. Brown
1947—J. Kramer
T. Brown
★1948—R. Falkenburg
J. E. Bromwich
1949—F. R. Schroeder
J. Drobny
★1950—B. Patty
F. A. Sedgman
1951—R. Savitt
K. McGregor
1952—F. A. Sedgman
J. Drobny
1953—V. Seixas
K. Nielsen
1954—J. Drobny
K. R. Rosewall
1955—T. Trabert
K. Nielsen
★1956—L. A. Hoad
K. R. Rosewall
1957—L. A. Hoad
A. J. Cooper
★1958—A. J. Cooper
N. A. Fraser
★1959—A. Olmedo
R. Laver
★1960—N. A. Fraser
R. Laver
1961—R. Laver
C. R. McKinley
1962—R. Laver
M. F. Mulligan

★1963—C. R. McKinley
F. S. Stolle
1964—R. Emerson
F. S. Stolle
1965—R. Emerson
F. S. Stolle
1966—M. Santana
R. D. Ralston
1967—J. D. Newcombe
W. P. Bungert
1968—R. Laver
A. D. Roche
1969—R. Laver
J. D. Newcombe
1970—J. D. Newcombe
K. R. Rosewall
1971—J. D. Newcombe
S. R. Smith
★1972—S. R. Smith
I. Nastase
★1973—J. Kodes
A. Metreveli
1974—J. S. Connors
K. R. Rosewall
1975—A. R. Ashe
J. S. Connors
1976—B. Borg
I. Nastase
1977—B. Borg
J. S. Connors
1978—B. Borg
J. S. Connors
1979—B. Borg
R. Tanner
1980—B. Borg
J. P. McEnroe
1981—J. P. McEnroe
B. Borg

1982—J. S. Connors
J. P. McEnroe
1983—J. P. McEnroe
C. J. Lewis
1984—J. P. McEnroe
J. S. Connors
1985—B. Becker
K. Curren
1986—B. Becker
I. Lendl
1987—P. Cash
I. Lendl
1988—S. Edberg
B. Becker
1989—B. Becker
S. Edberg
1990—S. Edberg
B. Becker
1991—M. Stich
B. Becker

MEN'S DOUBLES

1879—L. R. Erskine and H. F. Lawford
F. Durant and G. E. Tabor
1880—W. Renshaw and E. Renshaw
O. E. Woodhouse and C. J. Cole
1881—W. Renshaw and E. Renshaw
W. J. Down and H. Vaughan
1882—J. T. Hartley and R. T. Richardson
J. G. Horn and C. B. Russell
1883—C. W. Grinstead and C. E. Welldon
C. B. Russell and R. T. Milford
1884—W. Renshaw and E. Renshaw
E. W. Lewis and E. L. Williams
1885—W. Renshaw and E. Renshaw
C. E. Farrar and A. J. Stanley
1886—W. Renshaw and E. Renshaw
C. E. Farrar and A. J. Stanley
1887—P. Bowes-Lyon and H. W. W. Wilberforce
J. H. Crispe and Barratt Smith
1888—W. Renshaw and E. Renshaw
P. Bowes-Lyon and H. W. W. Wilberforce
1889—W. Renshaw and E. Renshaw
E. W. Lewis and G. W. Hillyard
1890—J. Pim and F. O. Stoker
E. W. Lewis and G. W. Hillyard
1891—W. Baddeley and H. Baddeley
J. Pim and F. O. Stoker
1892—H. S. Barlow and E. W. Lewis
W. Baddeley and H. Baddeley
1893—J. Pim and F. O. Stoker
E. W. Lewis and H. S. Barlow
1894—W. Baddeley and H. Baddeley
H. S. Barlow and C. H. Martin
1895—W. Baddeley and H. Baddeley
E. W. Lewis and W. V. Eaves
1896—W. Baddeley and H. Baddeley
R. F. Doherty and H. A. Nisbet
1897—R. F. Doherty and H. L. Doherty
W. Baddeley and H. Baddeley
1898—R. F. Doherty and H. L. Doherty
H. A. Nisbet and C. Hobart
1899—R. F. Doherty and H. L. Doherty
H. A. Nisbet and C. Hobart
1900—R. F. Doherty and H. L. Doherty
H. Roper Barrett and H. A. Nisbet
1901—R. F. Doherty and H. L. Doherty
Dwight Davis and Holcombe Ward
1902—S. H. Smith and F. L. Riseley
R. F. Doherty and H. L. Doherty
1903—R. F. Doherty and H. L. Doherty
S. H. Smith and F. L. Riseley
1904—R. F. Doherty and H. L. Doherty
S. H. Smith and F. L. Riseley
1905—R. F. Doherty and H. L. Doherty
S. H. Smith and F. L. Riseley
1906—S. H. Smith and F. L. Riseley
R. F. Doherty and H. L. Doherty
1907—N. E. Brookes and A. F. Wilding
B. C. Wright and K. Behr
1908—A. F. Wilding and M. J. G. Ritchie
A. W. Gore and H. Roper Barrett
1909—A. W. Gore and H. Roper Barrett
S. N. Doust and H. A. Parker
1910—A. F. Wilding and M. J. G. Ritchie
A. W. Gore and H. Roper Barrett
1911—M. Decugis and A. H. Gobert
M. J. G. Ritchie and A. F. Wilding
1912—H. Roper Barrett and C. P. Dixon
M. Decugis and A. H. Gobert

1913—H. Roper Barrett and C. P. Dixon
F. W. Rahe and H. Kleinschroth
1914—N. E. Brookes and A. F. Wilding
H. Roper Barrett and C. P. Dixon
1919—R. V. Thomas and P. O'Hara-Wood
R. Lycett and R. W. Heath
1920—R. N. Williams and C. S. Garland
A. R. F. Kingscote and J. C. Parke
1921—R. Lycett and M. Woosnam
F. G. Lowe and A. H. Lowe
†1922—R. Lycett and J. O. Anderson
G. L. Patterson and P. O'Hara-Wood
1923—R. Lycett and L. A. Godfree
Count de Gomar and E. Flaquer
1924—F. T. Hunter and V. Richards
R. N. Williams and W. M. Washburn
1925—J. Borotra and R. Lacoste
J. Hennessey and R. Casey
1926—H. Cochet and J. Brugnon
V. Richards and H. Kinsey
1927—F. T. Hunter and W. T. Tilden
J. Brugnon and H. Cochet
1928—H. Cochet and J. Brugnon
G. L. Patterson and J. B. Hawkes
1929—W. Allison and J. Van Ryn
J. C. Gregory and I. G. Collins
1930—W. Allison and J. Van Ryn
J. H. Doeg and G. M. Lott
1931—G. M. Lott and J. Van Ryn
H. Cochet and J. Brugnon
1932—J. Borotra and J. Brugnon
G. P. Hughes and F. J. Perry
1933—J. Borotra and J. Brugnon
R. Nunoi and J. Satoh
1934—G. M. Lott and L. R. Stoefen
J. Borotra and J. Brugnon
1935—J. H. Crawford and A. K. Quist
W. Allison and J. Van Ryn
1936—G. P. Hughes and C. R. D. Tuckey
C. E. Hare and F. H. D. Wilde
1937—J. D. Budge and G. Mako
G. P. Hughes and C. R. D. Tuckey
1938—J. D. Budge and G. Mako
H. Henkel and G. von Metaxa
1939—R. L. Riggs and E. T. Cooke
C. E. Hare and F. H. D. Wilde
1946—T. Brown and J. Kramer
G. E. Brown and D. Pails
1947—R. Falkenburg and J. Kramer
A. J. Mottram and O. W. Sidwell
1948—J. E. Bromwich and F. A. Sedgman
T. Brown and G. Mulloy
1949—R. Gonzales and F. Parker
G. Mulloy and F. R. Schroeder
1950—J. E. Bromwich and A. K. Quist
G. E. Brown and O. W. Sidwell
1951—K. McGregor and F. A. Sedgman
J. Drobny and E. W. Sturgess
1952—K. McGregor and F. A. Sedgman
V. Seixas and E. W. Sturgess
1953—L. A. Hoad and K. R. Rosewall
R. N. Hartwig and M. G. Rose
1954—R. N. Hartwig and M. G. Rose
V. Seixas and T. Trabert
1955—R. N. Hartwig and L. A. Hoad
N. A. Fraser and K. R. Rosewall
1956—L. A. Hoad and K. R. Rosewall
N. Pietrangeli and O. Sirola
1957—G. Mulloy and B. Patty
N. A. Fraser and L. A. Hoad

1958—S. Davidson and U. Schmidt
A. J. Cooper and N. A. Fraser
1959—R. Emerson and N. A. Fraser
R. Laver and R. Mark
1960—R. H. Osuna and R. D. Ralston
M. G. Davies and R. K. Wilson
1961—R. Emerson and N. A. Fraser
R. A. J. Hewitt and F. S. Stolle
1962—R. A. J. Hewitt and F. S. Stolle
B. Jovanovic and N. Pilic
1963—R. H. Osuna and A. Palafox
J. C. Barclay and P. Darmon
1964—R. A. J. Hewitt and F. S. Stolle
R. Emerson and K. N. Fletcher
1965—J. D. Newcombe and A. D. Roche
K. N. Fletcher and R. A. J. Hewitt
1966—K. N. Fletcher and J. D. Newcombe
W. W. Bowrey and O. K. Davidson
1967—R. A. J. Hewitt and F. D. McMillan
R. Emerson and K. N. Fletcher
1968—J. D. Newcombe and A. D. Roche
K. R. Rosewall and F. S. Stolle
1969—J. D. Newcombe and A. D. Roche
T. S. Okker and M. C. Riessen
1970—J. D. Newcombe and A. D. Roche
K. R. Rosewall and F. S. Stolle
1971—R. S. Emerson and R. G. Laver
A. R. Ashe and R. D. Ralston
1972—R. A. J. Hewitt and F. D. McMillan
S. R. Smith and E. J. van Dillen
1973—J. S. Connors and I. Nastase
J. R. Cooper and N. A. Fraser
1974—J. D. Newcombe and A. D. Roche
R. C. Lutz and S. R. Smith
1975—V. Gerulaitis and A. Mayer
C. Dowdeswell and A. J. Stone
1976—B. E. Gottfried and R. Ramirez
R. L. Case and G. Masters
1977—R. L. Case and G. Masters
J. G. Alexander and P. C. Dent
1978—R. A. J. Hewitt and F. D. McMillan
P. Fleming and J. P. McEnroe
1979—P. Fleming and J. P. McEnroe
B. E. Gottfried and R. Ramirez
1980—P. McNamara and P. McNamee
R. C. Lutz and S. R. Smith
1981—P. Fleming and J. P. McEnroe
R. C. Lutz and S. R. Smith
1982—P. McNamara and P. McNamee
P. Fleming and J. P. McEnroe
1983—P. Fleming and J. P. McEnroe
T. E. Gullikson and T. R. Gullikson
1984—P. Fleming and J. P. McEnroe
P. Cash and P. McNamee
1985—H. P. Guenthardt and B. Taroczy
P. Cash and J. B. Fitzgerald
1986—J. Nystrom and M. Wilander
G. Donnelly and P. Fleming
1987—K. Flach and R. Seguso
S. Casal and E. Sanchez
1988—K. Flach and R. Seguso
J. B. Fitzgerald and A. Jarryd
1989—J. B. Fitzgerald and A. Jarryd
R. Leach and J. Pugh
1990—R. Leach and J. Pugh
P. Aldrich and D. T. Visser
1991—J. B. Fitzgerald and A. Jarryd
J. Frana and L. Lavalle

THE CHAMPIONSHIP ROLL

LADIES' SINGLES

1884—Miss M. Watson
Miss Watson

1885—Miss M. Watson
Miss B. Bingley

1886—Miss B. Bingley
Miss M. Watson

1887—Miss L. Dod
Miss B. Bingley

1888—Miss L. Dod
Mrs. G. W. Hillyard

★1889—Mrs G. W. Hillyard
Miss L. Rice

★1890—Miss L. Rice
Miss Jacks

★1891—Miss L. Dod
Mrs. G. W. Hillyard

1892—Miss L. Dod
Mrs. G. W. Hillyard

1893—Miss L. Dod
Mrs. G. W. Hillyard

★1894—Mrs. G. W. Hillyard
Miss Austin

★1895—Miss C. Cooper
Miss Jackson

1896—Miss C. Cooper
Mrs. Pickering

1897—Mrs. G. W. Hillyard
Miss C. Cooper

★1898—Miss C. Cooper
Miss Martin

1899—Mrs. G. W. Hillyard
Miss C. Cooper

1900—Mrs. G. W. Hillyard
Miss C. Cooper

1901—Mrs. A. Sterry
Mrs. G. W. Hillyard

1902—Miss M. E. Robb
Mrs. A. Sterry

★1903—Miss D. K. Douglass
Miss E. W. Thomson

1904—Miss D. K. Douglass
Mrs. A. Sterry

1905—Miss M. Sutton
Miss D. K. Douglass

1906—Miss D. K. Douglass
Miss M. Sutton

1907—Miss M. Sutton
Mrs. Lambert Chambers

★1908—Mrs. A. Sterry
Miss A. M. Morton

★1909—Miss D. P. Boothby
Miss A. M. Morton

1910—Mrs. Lambert Chambers
Miss D. P. Boothby

1911—Mrs. Lambert Chambers
Miss D. P. Boothby

★1912—Mrs. D. R. Larcombe
Mrs. A. Sterry

★1913—Mrs. Lambert Chambers
Mrs. R. J. McNair

1914—Mrs. Lambert Chambers
Mrs. D. R. Larcombe

1919—Mlle. S. Lenglen
Mrs. Lambert Chambers

1920—Mlle S. Lenglen
Mrs. Lambert Chambers

1921—Mlle. S. Lenglen
Miss. E. Ryan

† 1922—Mlle. S. Lenglen
Mrs. Mallory

1923—Mlle. S. Lenglen
Miss K. McKane

1924—Miss K. McKane
Miss H. Wills

1925—Mlle. S. Lenglen
Miss J. Fry

1926—Mrs. L. A. Godfree
Sta. L. de Alvarez

1927—Miss H. Wills
Sta. L. de Alvarez

1928—Miss H. Wills
Sta. L. de Alvarez

1929—Miss H. Wills
Miss H. H. Jacobs

1930—Mrs. F. S. Moody
Miss E. Ryan

★1931—Fraulein C. Aussem
Fraulein H. Krahwinkel

1932—Mrs. F. S. Moody
Miss H. H. Jacobs

1933—Mrs. F. S. Moody
Miss D. E. Round

★1934—Miss D. E. Round
Miss H. H. Jacobs

1935—Mrs. F. S. Moody
Miss H. H. Jacobs

★1936—Miss H. H. Jacobs
Frau. S. Sperling

1937—Miss D. E. Round
Miss J. Jedrzeiowska

★1938—Mrs. F. S. Moody
Miss H. H. Jacobs

★1939—Miss A. Marble
Miss K. E. Stammers

★1946—Miss P. Betz
Miss L. Brough

★1947—Miss M. Osborne
Miss D. Hart

1948—Miss L. Brough
Miss D. Hart

1949—Miss L. Brough
Mrs. W. du Pont

1950—Miss L. Brough
Mrs. W. du Pont

1951—Miss D. Hart
Miss S. Fry

1952—Miss M. Connolly
Miss L. Brough

1953—Miss M. Connolly
Miss D. Hart

1954—Miss M. Connolly
Miss L. Brough

★1955—Miss L. Brough
Mrs. J. Fleitz

1956—Miss S. Fry
Miss A. Buxton

★1957—Miss A. Gibson
Miss D. R. Hard

1958—Miss A. Gibson
Miss A. Mortimer

★1959—Miss M. E. Bueno
Miss D. R. Hard

1960—Miss M. E. Bueno
Miss S. Reynolds

★1961—Miss A. Mortimer
Miss C. C. Truman

1962—Mrs. J. R. Susman
Mrs. V. Sukova

★1963—Miss M. Smith
Miss B. J. Moffitt

1964—Miss M. E. Bueno
Miss M. Smith

1965—Miss M. Smith
Miss M. E. Bueno

1966—Mrs. L. W. King
Miss M. E. Bueno

1967—Mrs. L. W. King
Mrs. P. F. Jones

1968—Mrs. L. W. King
Miss J. A. M. Tegart

1969—Mrs. P. F. Jones
Mrs. L. W. King

★1970—Mrs. B. M. Court
Mrs. L. W. King

1971—Miss E. F. Goolagong
Mrs. B. M. Court

1972—Mrs. L. W. King
Miss E. F. Goolagong

1973—Mrs. L. W. King
Miss C. M. Evert

1974—Miss C. M. Evert
Mrs. O. Morozova

1975—Mrs. L. W. King
Mrs. R. Cawley

★1976—Miss C. M. Evert
Mrs. R. Cawley

1977—Miss S. V. Wade
Miss B. F. Stove

1978—Miss M. Navratilova
Miss C. M. Evert

1979—Miss M. Navratilova
Mrs. J. M. Lloyd

1980—Mrs. R. Cawley
Mrs. J. M. Lloyd

1981—Mrs. J. M. Lloyd
Miss H. Mandlikova

1982—Miss M. Navratilova
Mrs. J. M. Lloyd

1983—Miss M. Navratilova
Miss A. Jaeger

1984—Miss M. Navratilova
Mrs. J. M. Lloyd

1985—Miss M. Navratilova
Mrs. J. M. Lloyd

1986—Miss M. Navratilova
Miss H. Mandlikova

1987—Miss M. Navratilova
Miss S. Graf

1988—Miss S. Graf
Miss M. Navratilova

1989—Miss S. Graf
Miss M. Navratilova

1990—Miss M. Navratilova
Miss Z. L. Garrison

1991—Miss S. Graf
Miss G. Sabatini

LADIES' DOUBLES

1913—Mrs. R. J. McNair and Miss D. P. Boothby
Mrs. A. Sterry and Mrs. Lambert Chambers

1914—Miss E. Ryan and Miss A. M. Morton
Mrs. D. R. Larcombe and Mrs. Hannam

1919—Mlle. S. Lenglen and Miss E. Ryan
Mrs. Lambert Chambers and Mrs. D. R. Larcombe

1920—Mlle. S. Lenglen and Miss E. Ryan
Mrs. Lambert Chambers and Mrs. D. R. Larcombe

1921—Mlle. S. Lenglen and Miss E. Ryan
Mrs. A. E. Beamish and Mrs. Peacock

1922—Mlle. S. Lenglen and Miss E. Ryan
Mrs. A. D. Stocks and Miss K. McKane

1923—Mlle. S. Lenglen and Miss E. Ryan
Miss J. Austin and Miss E. L. Colyer

1924—Mrs. H. Wightman and Miss H. Wills
Mrs. B. C. Covell and Miss K. McKane

1925—Mlle. S. Lenglen and Miss E. Ryan
Mrs. A. V. Bridge and Mrs. C. G. McIlquham

1926—Miss E. Ryan and Miss M. K. Browne
Mrs. L. A. Godfree and Miss E. L. Colyer

1927—Miss H. Wills and Miss E. Ryan
Miss E. L. Heine and Mrs. Peacock

1928—Mrs. Holcroft-Watson and Miss P. Saunders
Miss E. H. Harvey and Miss E. Bennett

1929—Mrs. Holcroft-Watson and Mrs. L. R. C. Michell
Mrs. B. C. Covell and Mrs. D. C. Shepherd-Barron

1930—Mrs. F. S. Moody and Miss E. Ryan
Miss E. Cross and Miss S. Palfrey

1931—Mrs. D. C. Shepherd-Barron and Miss P. E. Mudford
Mlle. D. Metaxa and Mlle. J. Sigart

1932—Mlle. D. Metaxa and Mlle. J. Sigart
Miss E. Ryan and Miss H. H. Jacobs

1933—Mme. R. Mathieu and Miss E. Ryan
Miss F. James and Miss A. M. Yorke

1934—Mme. R. Mathieu and Miss E. Ryan
Mrs. D. Andrus and Mme. Henrotin

1935—Miss F. James and Miss K. E. Stammers
Mme. R. Mathieu and Frau. S. Sperling

1936—Miss F. James and Miss K. E. Stammers
Mrs. S. P. Fabyan and Miss H. H. Jacobs

1937—Mme. R. Mathieu and Miss A. M. Yorke
Mrs. M. R. King and Mrs. J. B. Pittman

1938—Mrs. S. P. Fabyan and Miss A. Marble
Mme. R. Mathieu and Miss A. M. Yorke

1939—Mrs. S. P. Fabyan and Miss A. Marble
Miss H. H. Jacobs and Miss A. M. Yorke

1946—Miss L. Brough and Miss M. Osborne
Miss P. Betz and Miss D. Hart

1947—Miss D. Hart and Mrs. P. C. Todd
Miss L. Brough and Miss M. Osborne

1948—Miss L. Brough and Mrs W. du Pont
Miss D. Hart and Mrs. P. C. Todd

1949—Miss L. Brough and Mrs. W. du Pont
Miss G. Moran and Mrs. P. C. Todd

1950—Miss L. Brough and Mrs. W. du Pont
Miss S. Fry and Miss D. Hart

1951—Miss S. Fry and Miss D. Hart
Miss L. Brough and Mrs. W. du Pont

1952—Miss S. Fry and Miss D. Hart
Miss L. Brough and Miss M. Connolly

1953—Miss S. Fry and Miss D. Hart
Miss M. Connolly and Miss J. Sampson

1954—Miss L. Brough and Mrs. W. du Pont
Miss S. Fry and Miss D. Hart

1955—Miss A. Mortimer and Miss J. A. Shilcock
Miss S. J. Bloomer and Miss P. E. Ward

1956—Miss A. Buxton and Miss A. Gibson
Miss F. Muller and Miss D. G. Seeney

1957—Miss A. Gibson and Miss D. R. Hard
Mrs. K. Hawton and Mrs. T. D. Long

1958—Miss M. E. Bueno and Miss A. Gibson
Mrs. W. du Pont and Miss M. Varner

1959—Miss J. Arth and Miss D. R. Hard
Mrs. J. G. Fleitz and Miss C. C. Truman

1960—Miss M. E. Bueno and Miss D. R. Hard
Miss S. Reynolds and Miss R. Schuurman

1961—Miss K. Hantze and Miss B. J. Moffitt
Miss J. Lehane and Miss M. Smith

1962—Miss B. J. Moffitt and Mrs. J. R. Susman
Mrs. L. E. G. Price and Miss R. Schuurman

1963—Miss M. E. Bueno and Miss D. R. Hard
Miss R. A. Ebbern and Miss M. Smith

1964—Miss M. Smith and Miss L. R. Turner
Miss B. J. Moffitt and Mrs. J. R. Susman

1965—Miss M. E. Bueno and Miss B. J. Moffitt
Miss F. Durr and Miss J. Lieffrig

1966—Miss M. E. Bueno and Miss N. Richey
Miss M. Smith and Miss J. A. M. Tegart

1967—Miss R. Casals and Mrs. L. W. King
Miss M. E. Bueno and Miss N. Richey

1968—Miss R. Casals and Mrs. L. W. King
Miss F. Durr and Mrs. P. F. Jones

1969—Mrs. B. M. Court and Miss J. A. M. Tegart
Miss P. S. A. Hogan and Miss M. Michel

1970—Miss R. Casals and Mrs. L. W. King
Miss F. Durr and Miss S. V. Wade

1971—Miss R. Casals and Mrs. L. W. King
Mrs. B. M. Court and Miss E. F. Goolagong

1972—Mrs. L. W. King and Miss B. F. Stove
Mrs. D. E. Dalton and Miss F. Durr

1973—Miss R. Casals and Mrs. L. W. King
Miss F. Durr and Miss B. F. Stove

1974—Miss E. F. Goolagong and Miss M. Michel
Miss H. F. Gourlay and Miss K. M. Krantzcke

1975—Miss A. K. Kiyomura and Miss K. Sawamatsu
Miss F. Durr and Miss B. F. Stove

1976—Miss C. M. Evert and Miss M. Navratilova
Mrs. L. W. King and Miss B. F. Stove

1977—Mrs. H. F. Gourlay Cawley and Miss J. C. Russell
Miss M. Navratilova and Miss B. F. Stove

1978—Mrs. G. E. Reid and Miss W. M. Turnbull
Miss M. Jausovec and Miss V. Ruzici

1979—Mrs. L. W. King and Miss M. Navratilova
Miss B. F. Stove and Miss W. M. Turnbull

1980—Miss K. Jordan and Miss A. E. Smith
Miss R. Casals and Miss W. M. Turnbull

1981—Miss M. Navratilova and Miss P. H. Shriver
Miss K. Jordan and Miss A. E. Smith

1982—Miss M. Navratilova and Miss P. H. Shriver
Miss K. Jordan and Miss A. E. Smith

1983—Miss M. Navratilova and Miss P. H. Shriver
Miss R. Casals and Miss W. M. Turnbull

1984—Miss M. Navratilova and Miss P. H. Shriver
Miss K. Jordan and Miss A. E. Smith

1985—Miss K. Jordan and Mrs. P. D. Smylie
Miss M. Navratilova and Miss P. H. Shriver

1986—Miss M. Navratilova and Miss P. H. Shriver
Miss H. Mandlikova and Miss W. M. Turnbull

1987—Miss C. Kohde-Kilsch and Miss H. Sukova
Miss B. Nagelsen and Mrs. P. D. Smylie

1988—Miss S. Graf and Miss G. Sabatini
Miss L. Savchenko and Miss N. Zvereva

1989—Miss J. Novotna and Miss H. Sukova
Miss L. Savchenko and Miss N. Zvereva

1990—Miss J. Novotna and Miss H. Sukova
Miss K. Jordan and Mrs. P. D. Smylie

1991—Miss L. Savchenko and Miss N. Zvereva
Miss G. Fernandez and Miss J. Novotna

MAIDEN NAMES OF LADY CHAMPIONS

In the above tables the following have been recorded in both married and single identities.

Mrs. R. Cawley	Miss E. F. Goolagong	*Mrs. G. W. Hillyard*	Miss B. Bingley	*Mrs. L. E. G. Price*	Miss S. Reynolds
Mrs. Lambert Chambers	Miss D. K. Douglass	*Mrs. P. F. Jones*	Miss A. S. Haydon	*Mrs. G. E. Reid*	Miss K. Melville
Mrs. B. M. Court	Miss M. Smith	*Mrs. L. W. King*	Miss B. J. Moffitt	*Mrs. P. D. Smylie*	Miss E. M. Sayers
Mrs. B. C. Covell	Miss P. L. Howkins	*Mrs. M. R. King*	Miss P. E. Mudford	*Frau. S. Sperling*	Fraulein H. Krahwinkel
Mrs. D. E. Dalton	Miss J. A. M. Tegart	*Mrs. D. R. Larcombe*	Miss E. W. Thomson	*Mrs. A. Sterry*	Miss C. Cooper
Mrs. W. du Pont	Miss M. Osborne	*Mrs. J. M. Lloyd*	Miss C. M. Evert	*Mrs. J. R. Susman*	Miss K. Hantze
Mrs. L. A. Godfree	Miss K. McKane	*Mrs. F. S. Moody*	Miss H. Wills		
Mrs. H. F. Gourlay Cawley	Miss H. F. Gourlay	*Mrs. O. Morozova*	Miss O. Morozova		

NOTE.—For the years 1913, 1914 and 1919-1923 inclusive the above records include the "World's Championship on Grass" granted to The Lawn Tennis Association by The International Lawn Tennis Federation. This title was then abolished and commencing in 1924 they became The Official Lawn Tennis Championships recognised by The International Lawn Tennis Federation.

Prior to 1922 the holders in the Singles Events and Gentlemen's Doubles did not compete in the Championships but met the winners of these events in the Challenge Rounds.

†Challenge Round abolished: holders subsequently played through. ★*The holder did not defend the title.*

THE CHAMPIONSHIP ROLL

MIXED DOUBLES

1913—Hope Crisp and Mrs. C. O. Tuckey
J. C. Parke and Mrs. D. R. Larcombe
1914—J. C. Parke and Mrs. D. R. Larcombe
A. F. Wilding and Mlle. Broquedis
1919—R. Lycett and Miss E. Ryan
A. D. Prebble and Mrs. Lambert Chambers
1920—G. L. Patterson and Mlle. S. Lenglen
R. Lycett and Miss E. Ryan
1921—R. Lycett and Miss E. Ryan
M. Woosnam and Miss P. L. Howkins
1922—P. O'Hara-Wood and Mlle. S. Lenglen
R. Lycett and Miss E. Ryan
1923—R. Lycett and Miss E. Ryan
L. S. Deane and Mrs. D. C. Shepherd-Barron
1924—J. B. Gilbert and Miss K. McKane
L. A. Godfree and Mrs. D. C. Shepherd-Barron
1925—J. Borotra and Mlle. S. Lenglen
H. L. de Morpurgo and Miss E. Ryan
1926—L. A. Godfree and Mrs. L. A. Godfree
H. Kinsey and Miss M. K. Browne
1927—F. T. Hunter and Miss E. Ryan
L. A. Godfree and Mrs. L. A. Godfree
1928—P. D. B. Spence and Miss E. Ryan
J. Crawford and Miss D. Akhurst
1929—F. T. Hunter and Miss H. Wills
I. G. Collins and Miss J. Fry
1930—J. H. Crawford and Miss E. Ryan
D. Prenn and Fraulein H. Krahwinkel
1931—G. M. Lott and Mrs. L. A. Harper
I. G. Collins and Miss J. C. Ridley
1932—E. Maier and Miss E. Ryan
H. C. Hopman and Mlle. J. Sigart
1933—G. von Cramm and Fraulein H. Krahwinkel
N. G. Farquharson and Miss M. Heeley
1934—R. Miki and Miss D. E. Round
H. W. Austin and Mrs. D. C. Shepherd-Barron
1935—F. J. Perry and Miss D. E. Round
H. C. Hopman and Mrs. H. C. Hopman
1936—F. J. Perry and Miss D. E. Round
J. D. Budge and Mrs. S. P. Fabyan
1937—J. D. Budge and Miss A. Marble
Y. Petra and Mme. R. Mathieu
1938—J. D. Budge and Miss A. Marble
H. Henkel and Mrs. S. P. Fabyan
1939—R. L. Riggs and Miss A. Marble
F. H. D. Wilde and Miss N. B. Brown

1946—T. Brown and Miss L. Brough
G. E. Brown and Miss D. Bundy
1947—J. E. Bromwich and Miss L. Brough
C. F. Long and Mrs. N. M. Bolton
1948—J. E. Bromwich and Miss L. Brough
F. A. Sedgman and Miss D. Hart
1949—E. W. Sturgess and Mrs. S. P. Summers
J. E. Bromwich and Miss L. Brough
1950—E. W. Sturgess and Miss L. Brough
G. E. Brown and Mrs. P. C. Todd
1951—F. A. Sedgman and Miss D. Hart
M. G. Rose and Mrs. N. M. Bolton
1952—F. A. Sedgman and Miss D. Hart
E. Morea and Mrs. T. D. Long
1953—V. Seixas and Miss D. Hart
E. Morea and Miss S. Fry
1954—V. Seixas and Miss D. Hart
K. R. Rosewall and Mrs. W. du Pont
1955—V. Seixas and Miss D. Hart
E. Morea and Miss L. Brough
1956—V. Seixas and Miss S. Fry
G. Mulloy and Mrs. L. A. Godfree
1957—M. G. Rose and Miss D. R. Hard
N. A. Fraser and Miss A. Gibson
1958—R. N. Howe and Miss L. Coghlan
K. Nielsen and Miss A. Gibson
1959—R. Laver and Miss D. R. Hard
N. A. Fraser and Miss M. E. Bueno
1960—R. Laver and Miss D. R. Hard
R. N. Howe and Miss M. E. Bueno
1961—F. S. Stolle and Miss L. R. Turner
R. N. Howe and Miss E. Bu'ing
1962—N. A. Fraser and Mrs. W. du Pont
R. D. Ralston and Miss A. S. Haydon
1963—K. N. Fletcher and Miss M. Smith
R. A. J. Hewitt and Miss D. R. Hard
1964—F. S. Stolle and Miss L. R. Turner
K. N. Fletcher and Miss M. Smith
1965—K. N. Fletcher and Miss M. Smith
A. D. Roche and Miss J. A. M. Tegart
1966—K. N. Fletcher and Miss M. Smith
R. D. Ralston and Mrs. L. W. King
1967—O. K. Davidson and Mrs. L. W. King
K. N. Fletcher and Miss M. Smith
1968—K. N. Fletcher and Mrs. B. M. Court
A. Metreveli and Miss O. Morozova

1969—F. S. Stolle and Mrs. P. F. Jones
A. D. Roche and Miss J. A. M. Tegart
1970—I. Nastase and Miss R. Casals
A. Metreveli and Miss O. Morozova
1971—O. K. Davidson and Mrs. L. W. King
M. C. Riessen and Mrs. B. M. Court
1972—I. Nastase and Miss R. Casals
K. G. Warwick and Miss E. F. Goolagong
1973—O. K. Davidson and Mrs. L. W. King
R. Ramirez and Miss J. S. Newberry
1974—O. K. Davidson and Mrs. L. W. King
M. J. Farrell and Miss L. J. Charles
1975—M. C. Riessen and Mrs. B. M. Court
A. J. Stone and Miss B. F. Stove
1976—A. D. Roche and Miss F. Durr
R. L. Stockton and Miss R. Casals
1977—R. A. J. Hewitt and Miss G. R. Stevens
F. D. McMillan and Miss B. F. Stove
1978—F. D. McMillan and Miss B. F. Stove
R. O. Ruffels and Mrs. L. W. King
1979—R. A. J. Hewitt and Miss G. R. Stevens
F. D. McMillan and Miss B. F. Stove
1980—J. R. Austin and Miss T. Austin
M. R. Edmondson and Miss D. L. Fromholtz
1981—F. D. McMillan and Miss B. F. Stove
J. R. Austin and Miss T. Austin
1982—K. Curren and Miss A. E. Smith
J. M. Lloyd and Miss W. M. Turnbull
1983—J. M. Lloyd and Miss W. M. Turnbull
S. Denton and Mrs. L. W. King
1984—J. M. Lloyd and Miss W. M. Turnbull
S. Denton and Miss K. Jordan
1985—P. McNamee and Miss M. Navratilova
J. B. Fitzgerald and Mrs. P. D. Smylie
1986—K. Flach and Miss K. Jordan
H. P. Guenthardt and Miss M. Navratilova
1987—M. J. Bates and Miss J. M. Durie
D. Cahill and Miss N. Provis
1988—S. E. Stewart and Miss Z. L. Garrison
K. Jones and Mrs. S. W. Magers
1989—J. Pugh and Miss J. Novotna
M. Kratzmann and Miss J. M. Byrne
1990—R. Leach and Miss Z. L. Garrison
J. B. Fitzgerald and Mrs. P. D. Smylie
1991—J. B. Fitzgerald and Mrs. P. D. Smylie
J. Pugh and Miss N. Zvereva

THE JUNIORS CHAMPIONSHIP ROLL

BOYS' SINGLES

1948—S. Stockenberg (Sweden)
1949—S. Stockenberg (Sweden)
1950—J. A. T. Horn (G.B.)
1951—J. Kupferburger (S.A.)
1952—R. K. Wilson (G.B.)
1953—W. A. Knight (G.B.)
1954—R. Krishnan (India)
1955—M. P. Hann (G.B.)
1956—R. Holmberg (U.S.A.)
1957—J. I. Tattersall (G.B.)
1958—E. Buchholz (U.S.A.)

1959—T. Lejus (U.S.S.R.)
1960—A. R. Mandelstam (S.A.)
1961—C. E. Graebner (U.S.A.)
1962—S. Matthews (G.B.)
1963—N. Kalogeropoulos (Greece)
1964—I. El Shafei (U.A.R.)
1965—V. Korotkov (U.S.S.R.)
1966—V. Korotkov (U.S.S.R.)
1967—M. Orantes (Spain)
1968—J. G. Alexander (Australia)
1969—B. Bertram (S.A.)

1970—B. Bertram (S.A.)
1971—R. Kreiss (U.S.A.)
1972—B. Borg (Sweden)
1973—W. Martin (U.S.A.)
1974—W. Martin (U.S.A.)
1975—C. J. Lewis (N.Z.)
1976—H. Guenthardt (Switzerland)
1977—V. A. Winitsky (U.S.A.)
1978—I. Lendl (Czechoslovakia)
1979—R. Krishnan (India)
1980—T. Tulasne (France)

1981—M. W. Anger (U.S.A.)
1982—P. Cash (Australia)
1983—S. Edberg (Sweden)
1984—M. Kratzmann (Australia)
1985—L. Lavalle (Mexico)
1986—E. Velez (Mexico)
1987—D. Nargisco (Italy)
1988—N. Pereira (Venezuela)
1989—N. Kulti (Sweden)
1990—L. Paes (India)
1991—T. Enqvist (Sweden)

BOYS' DOUBLES

1982—P. Cash and J. Frawley
1983—M. Kratzmann and S. Youl
1984—R. Brown and R. Weiss

1985—A. Moreno and J. Yzaga
1986—T. Carbonnell and P. Korda
1987—J. Stoltenberg and T. Woodbridge
1988—J. Stoltenberg and T. Woodbridge

1989—J. Palmer and J. Stark
1990—S. Lareau and S. Leblanc
1991—K. Alami and G. Rusedski

GIRLS' SINGLES

1948—Miss O. Miskova (Czechoslovakia)
1949—Miss C. Mercelis (Belgium)
1950—Miss L. Cornell (G.B.)
1951—Miss L. Cornell (G.B.)
1952—Miss ten Bosch (Netherlands)
1953—Miss D. Kilian (S.A.)
1954—Miss V. A. Pitt (G.B.)
1955—Miss S. M. Armstrong (G.B.)
1956—Miss A. S. Haydon (G.B.)
1957—Miss M. Arnold (U.S.A.)
1958—Miss S. M. Moore (U.S.A.)

1959—Miss J. Cross (S.A.)
1960—Miss K. Hantze (U.S.A.)
1961—Miss G. Baksheeva (U.S.S.R.)
1962—Miss G. Baksheeva (U.S.S.R.)
1963—Miss D. M. Salfati (France)
1964—Miss P. Bartkowicz (U.S.A.)
1965—Miss O. Morozova (U.S.S.R.)
1966—Miss B. Lindstrom (Finland)
1967—Miss J. Salome (Netherlands)
1968—Miss K. Pigeon (U.S.A.)
1969—Miss K. Sawamatsu (Japan)

1970—Miss S. Walsh (U.S.A.)
1971—Miss M. Kroschina (U.S.S.R.)
1972—Miss I. Kloss (S.A.)
1973—Miss A. Kiyomura (U.S.A.)
1974—Miss M Jausovec (Yugoslavia)
1975—Miss N. Y. Chmyreva (U.S.S.R.)
1976—Miss N. Y. Chmyreva (U.S.S.R.)
1977—Miss L. Antonoplis (U.S.A.)
1978—Miss T. Austin (U.S.A.)
1979—Miss M. L. Piatek (U.S.A.)
1980—Miss D. Freeman (Australia)

1981—Miss Z. Garrison (U.S.A.)
1982—Miss C. Tanvier (France)
1983—Miss P. Paradis (France)
1984—Miss A. N. Croft (G.B.)
1985—Miss A. Holikova (Czechoslovakia)
1986—Miss N. Zvereva (U.S.S.R.)
1987—Miss N. Zvereva (U.S.S.R.)
1988—Miss B. Schultz (Netherlands)
1989—Miss A. Strnadova (Czechoslovakia)
1990—Miss A. Strnadova (Czechoslovakia)
1991—Miss B. Rittner (Germany)

GIRLS' DOUBLES

1982—Miss B. Herr and Miss P. Barg
1983—Miss P. Fendick and Miss P. Hy
1984—Miss C. Kuhlman and Miss S. Rehe

1985—Miss L. Field and Miss J. Thompson
1986—Miss M. Jaggard and Miss L. O'Neill
1987—Miss N. Medvedeva and Miss N. Zvereva
1988—Miss J.-A. Faull and Miss R. McQuillan

1989—Miss J. Capriati and Miss M. McGrath
1990—Miss K. Habsudova and Miss A. Strnadova
1991—Miss C. Barclay and Miss L. Zaltz